DEACON'S DISSENTERS RAISE THE CROSS

THE HISTO[illegible]OIRS OF CROSS H[illegible]URCH

CROSS HILLS UNITED RESEARCHED CHURCH HISTORY

(C.H.U.R.C.H.)

Committee Members:

Chairman: Frank Gregory

Secretary: Bessie Willett

Treasurer: Peter Willett

Yvonne Gregory: Ida Gregory;

Robert Holmes; Pastor Garry Kelly.

by

Frank Gregory

&

Peter Willett

CATAMOUNT PUBLICATIONS

1998

Artwork on cover: Victoria Brookland

Photographic reproduction: Stephen Bloomfield

ISBN 0 9526718 2 4

Printed in Great Britain by:

RURAL PRESS LTD

1a Shirley Street

Leicester LE4 5JT

Published by:

CATAMOUNT PUBLICATIONS

288 Station Road

Bagworth

COALVILLE

Leicestershire.

LE67 1BN

THIS BOOK IS DEDICATED TO:

The many members at Cross Hills who are NOT mentioned in this book. Throughout the years, from 1796 the Church has been served valiantly by ordinary Christian men and women who dedicated themselves to work for Cross Hills and the 'Glory of God', giving all they had throughout hardship and persecution in the early days— many never holding office, these are the Cross Hills 'unknown warriors'.

But as John writes in Revelation, Chapter 7. V.14. *'These are they which came out of great tribulation, and have washed their robes and made them white in the blood of the lamb.'*

We know them not, but their names are written in the 'Lambs book of Life'.

And to the memory of:

my mother, Mrs. Emma Willett, 1901 - 1985, who through 43 years of her life was deprived of her health and strength to work for Cross Hills. However, she did what she could by passing on to me most of the stories that you will read in this book.

Peter Willett

To Ida Gregory, a wonderful wife and mother, enduring all my moods, believing in me at times when I hardly believed in myself, inspiring, encouraging in the 'darkest hours'. And for giving Yvonne Dawn Gregory, our daughter, the special love and care she needed to survive, and which no other person in the world, professional or otherwise, could have possibly given.

Frank Gregory

About the authors:

Frank Gregory lives in Bagworth and is a retired British Coal employee, who worked at nearby Desford colliery for nearly 27 years until shortly before it closed in 1984. He worked both underground and on the surface as a supervisory mechanic. When the coal seams became difficult and uneconomic to work, and the pit closure programme claimed Desford pit, he preferred to take redundancy and pursue a lifetime ambition of writing, rather than take the uncertain option of moving out of the area away from friends and family.

Realising the advantages of learning to type and to use computer operated word processors, Frank bought a computer in the early 80's and set about teaching himself how to use it with the invaluable help of fellow writer, Steve Duckworth. Frank is also forever indebted to Coun. Stephen Peace of the Springboard Centre, Coalville, who so willingly offers his advice and professionalism and is always a great help and encouragement.

Specialising in local history and local news, Frank has been published widely in the Leicester Mercury and other publications since the mid 1980's. In 1995 he became particularly interested in the history of Cross Hills church, just prior to the new building being erected. During the transition period between the demolition of the old church and the building of the new, some services had to be temporarily held at Bagworth community centre. After attending several services in the makeshift church, his nose for sniffing out history could be contained no longer. On the evening of March 21st 1997 he first approached Peter Willett, a deacon and Treasurer of Cross Hills church, about the possibility of jointly researching the history, and producing a permanent unique record for the benefit of future generations and archives. Consequently, a group was formed and the challenge began to research the book through to the finished publication.

From this brief two-minute phone call evolved the basis of the book in your hands, which is the result of over a year of intense and painstaking research. All of which was a pleasure, he says, because of the added bonus of discovering in parallel a hard working and valuable friend in Peter Willett.

About the authors:

Peter Willett was born in 1932 at Little Bagworth in one of a group of 13 houses in Heath Road, all now demolished through mining subsidence damage.

His father, George Willett, a coal and haulage contractor and his mother, Emma Willett (nee Prime) were members at Cross Hills, and both of their families had very strong connections at the church since before 1910. Peter therefore had a good start at Cross Hills and can remember quite clearly being carried up the stairs in the chapel by his grandfather (William Prime, the Choirmaster) in 1935 to see the 'new' organ being installed, and also standing on the seats during choir practice between his mother and other members, to sing at the age of 3 years.

This must have sparked off his interest in singing, which has remained for the rest of his life.

He attended Sunday School from 4 years of age, was baptized and joined the Church at 17 years, taught in the Sunday School for 14 years and was made a deacon in 1967. In 1996 he was made a life deacon in recognition of his work and supervision as Chairman of the Building Committee during the planning and building of the 'new church'.

He started work underground at Bagworth colliery in 1948, married his wife Bessie in 1958 and they have two children. Bessie has been a Sunday School teacher at Cross Hills for 22 years and a deacon for many years also.

Peter qualified as a mine surveyor in 1960 and worked for the National Coal Board at several collieries in the area. In 1971 he worked for 4 years as a Civil Engineering Technician with Leicester City Corporation, but returned to the National Coal Board for the last 11 years of his working life.

His main hobbies throughout his life have been tennis, badminton, photography, DIY, furniture restoration and in particular, singing. He has been a member of Broom Leys Choral Society for the last 13 years.

Now that Cross Hills has a new church, his desire is to see the Lord's work continue to grow there and prosper, as it has from the day that it was completed.

FOREWORD

by Reverend Bernard Green M.A. B.D.

I have read this book with great interest, and congratulate Frank Gregory and Peter Willett on producing such a fascinating account of the Cross Hills Baptist Church's story. It is a good story, worthy of being widely read. It is also a timely reminder that God works through not only large churches and famous people, but in many small places and through countless ordinary people who dedicate themselves with persevering faith to the cause of Christ.

How appropriate it is that the book is dedicated to the many members at Cross Hills who are not mentioned in it, as well as to the memory of two devoted women — one a mother and the other a wife of the two authors. Since the open-air gospel preaching in Bagworth in 1796 and the subsequent growth of Baptist witness as an outreach of the historic Barton Fabis Baptist Church, generation after generation of local families have been blessed and used by God. The book records the view of a Professor of History at Exeter University, Nicholas Orme, a descendant of one of the families involved with Cross Hills for many years: *'I certainly think that the Baptist Movement has played an important part in the social history of Bagworth/Thornton, as well as the religious history of the area....'* That underlines the significance of the congregations, large and small, which gather regularly in our church buildings week by week, year by year.

Times, of course, have changed. The old collieries have gone and patterns of life are radically different. Church programmes and methods today would have amazed, perhaps even shocked, our forefathers. But the Christian gospel still speaks to the basic needs of all sorts of people. And God is ready to work through Christians who are committed to a way of being the church which witnesses and serves in the world around it.

As a new century approaches, the Christian Church worldwide is trying to discern God's purposes for the future. The company of believers at Cross Hills, with their attractive new premises and with the story of this book to inspire them, can face the future with confidence. I hope and pray that they will serve tomorrow's community as their spiritual ancestors faithfully served their neighbourhood in the past. Then the church, which at one time seemed to have been built in no-man's-land, will in fact be on the main road of the Kingdom of God.

Bernard Green

(Former General Secretary of the Baptist Union of Great Britain)

INTRODUCTION

This is the fascinating story of one small Baptist church, teeming with history, set in a few square metres of land in one tiny corner of Leicestershire. Cross Hills Baptist Church was built not in a town or village, as might be termed 'conventional', but in 'no-man's-land'. It is set midway between two villages, on a steep hill and a sharp bend.

On at least one occasion the hidden site of Cross Hills caused a little anxiety to a young Lay Preacher. Mr. L.T. Childs, of Measham, was cycling over to take his first service and was awaited by the Deacons outside the church to greet him. Unfortunately, the Force of Gravity had taken the initiative and Mr. Childs found himself whizzing by his destination to the dismay of his reception party. One could imagine it would by quite some minutes before the unfortunate young Lay Preacher could retrace his path up the steep road and allay his embarrassment. **(See chapter 24)**

Why are churches like Cross Hills — and I have heard stories that there are quite a few around the country — built in isolation in the countryside? You will find the answer in this book.

Remember that original Baptist churches were built when motor cars were nonexistent. The best thing you could hope for was to travel by horse and trap if the distance was great or, as was more usual, the mode of transport was 'Shanks's Pony'. Without exception, the pioneering preachers walked many miles daily to spread the Word. Week after week these dedicated men trudged around Wales, England, Charnwood Forest and its many towns and villages, preaching to the crowds, often arriving back home at 3am.

It is approaching 260 years now since the first brave Baptist preachers arrived in the area, making their Headquarters at Barton in the Beans. They were attacked, outlawed and humiliated by people who were so-called 'members' of the conventional church, people who called themselves Christians. The preachers' houses were ransacked and vandalised, their families dragged through all the filth their tormentors could find. They were pelted with dung, had their clothes ripped off their backs. At times these dedicated pioneers were subjected to the very brink of death.

What brave and valiant people these men and women were. Never giving up, spreading the Word and establishing ever more Baptist churches, until they were finally accepted into society by 'supporters' of the Anglican church. Even though, often, that acceptance was by Law enforcement: it was seldom voluntary.

The story of the Great Awakening, of the Evangelical Revival and the evolution of the New Connexion of General Baptists, is a story of brave, dedicated preachers. It is a story that has been told in great detail in other volumes. We have given but a condensed version at the front of the book to weave in the local connection. Our story is about one small church, on the edge of Charnwood Forest. That church is Cross Hills, with its wealth of fascinating characters. The difficulties encountered, the triumphs mastered; colourful ceremonies and concerts; Sunday school anniversaries and sermons' days, etc.

In 1996 a new building was erected to replace the subsidence riddled old building. This is the third church built on the same small plot of land.

The new church is light and bright and uplifting to the spirit. Upon entering, I find there is a wonderful feeling of peace and love, a feeling which has also been echoed by others not accustomed to worshipping in the church regularly. Cross Hills is a house of God, where we give our thanks and prayers to Him. But even to a stranger on a casual visit, there is that certain bright and breezy atmosphere which somehow penetrates and pervades well beyond the realms of bricks and mortar. Every window, each sliver of polished wood, seems to vibrate with life. The Petal Window, which has survived the demolition hammer in the old church, is still shining God's light on us so brightly in the new. And most important of all, it is the people who come to praise God who make this church come to life so vividly.

My heartfelt thanks go out to my co-author and Treasurer of Cross Hills, Mr. Peter Willett for his tremendous efforts in tracing stories of many old characters, and photographs, past and present. He has been, and is, one of the mainstays of the church, having so many skills and executing some of the countless essential 'backroom boy' jobs that the congregation seldom know of. To him I take my hat off. He is the third generation in his family to consecutively take on the Treasurer's job, covering an unbroken service of almost the whole of the 20th century. That is a wonderful record, I know you will all agree.

Finally, I hope you enjoy exploring this book, the research and writing of which has been the greatest pleasure for both Peter and myself. The pace of Peter's untiring delving into Cross Hills past history almost leaves me breathless— but very, very grateful; capturing those heartwarming little stories that would otherwise be lost to our descendants for ever. Our wish is that this book fills a rightful place in local, County and Baptist Church history for the benefit of generations to come. So many important memories go to the grave without being properly recorded: our earnest hope is that we have filled just one tiny gap.

Frank Gregory

ACKNOWLEDGEMENTS

This book has been kindly sponsored by the following bodies:

Artscope, a Calouste Gulbenkian Foundation rural arts agency, managed by Mantle Arts.

Bagworth Parish Council.

Leicestershire Coalfields Rural Initiative Funds.

Leicestershire County Council – Community Education Office.

Markfield Plastics – Station Rd, Bagworth 01530 230496

Midland Co-operative Society, Limited.

Dunlop Ltd: Precision Rubbers Division

R.J.H. Building Construction Ltd 01530 834040

Caterpillar U.K. Ltd.

Gordon Buchanan – High Class Butcher

E.J. & K.A. Orme – Budget Boiler Services 01530 230631

Garry Kelly – Miss Print 01455 616844

Robert Talbott – Moruplast Ltd, Injection Mould Toolmakers 01530 242477

Tom Underwood – Ibstock Electrical 01530 260543

Mr R. & Mrs C. Miles, Poplar House farm, Bagworth

Mr D.A. Hunting, Bagworth

J.E. Brown, Manor Farm, Thornton 01530 230432

Robert Savage, Market Bosworth – Builder 01455 290474

Gillivers – Funeral Directors – Barlestone 01455 290356

Damien Barks, Linda Barks and Brian Barks

The Smith Family, Thornton Nurseries 01530 230331

For Information and Help

Professor Nicholas Orme, of Exeter University.

Dr. Harold Fox, of Leicester University.

Mr. & Mrs. D. Meller, for access to the Barton Archives.

Edward & Karen Orme, for the loan of family photographs, etc.

Mr .Geoff. Tovell of Hugglescote

and all who contributed photo's & information.

Thank you Peter. Thank you Bessie. Thank you for the many hours of hospitality shown to me and the welcome into your home, the countless cups of resuscitative liquid administered— of the caffeine variety, I hasten to add— while researching for this book.

Also, many thanks to my daughter, Yvonne Gregory, first Secretary of our Group who, despite her serious health problems and her commitment to pursuing a part-time B.A. honours degree course in English Literature at Loughborough University, spent many hours in the furtherance of this book in its early stages.

A special thank you to Bessie Willett for taking over at short notice as our Second Secretary , and adding her special expertise to our project.

Frank Gregory

CONTENTS

PART I: PRE-CROSS HILLS DAYS

PART II: THE FIRST CROSS HILLS BAPTIST CHAPEL

PART III: THE SECOND CROSS HILLS BAPTIST CHAPEL

PART IV: MUSIC AND SUNDAY SCHOOL

PART V: CROSS HILLS GOES WORLD WIDE

PART VI: OFFICERS OF THE CHURCH

PART VII: MINING SUBSIDENCE

PART VIII: VISIONS OF A NEW CHURCH

PART IX: BUILDING CROSS HILLS BAPTIST CHURCH NUMBER THREE

Where on Earth are the Villages of Bagworth, Thornton & Barton-in-the-Beans?

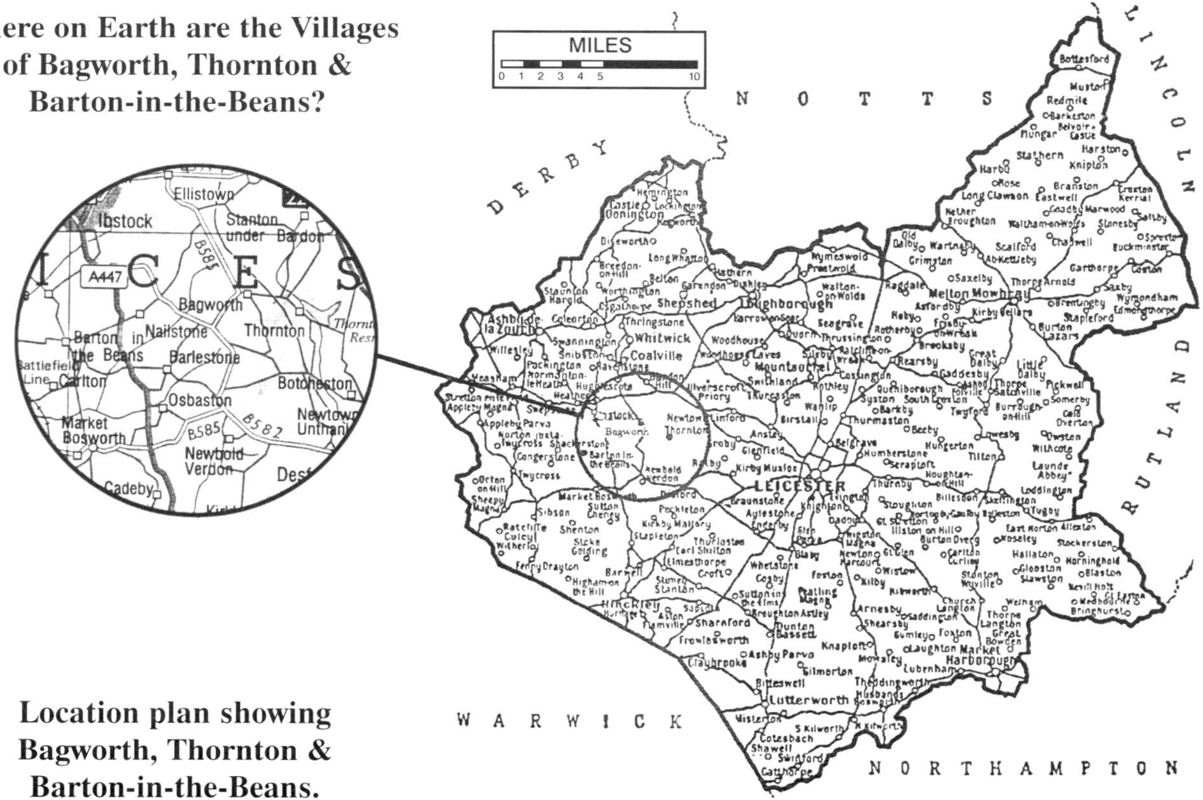

Location plan showing Bagworth, Thornton & Barton-in-the-Beans.

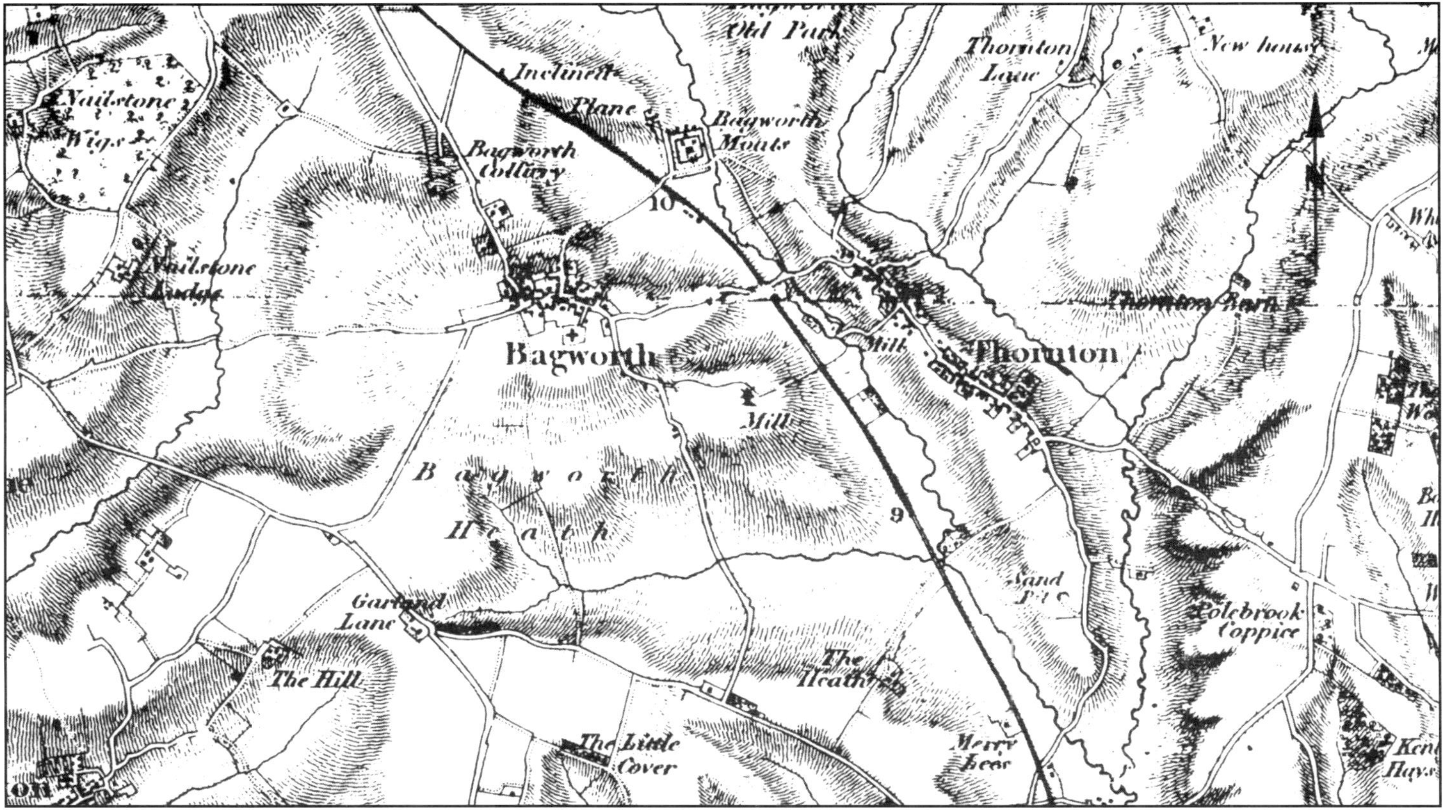

1835 map showing Bagworth & Thornton villages with 'The Moats', the old park, Bagworth Heath and Stephenson's Swannington — Leicester railway. Scale approx. 2 ins. to 1 mile.

PART I: PRE-CROSS HILLS DAYS

CHAPTER 1

BRIEF HISTORY OF BAGWORTH AND THORNTON VILLAGES

Land is seized by nobility

The Church, whether it be Church of England or Nonconformist, is the body of the people who worship God. It is not only the building in which they meet for worship. **This short historical section has been included to show the plight of the people prior to the time when the Baptist Movement evolved.**

The majority of village life in this country revolved around the Manor, and Bagworth and Thornton were no exception. Most of the ground and cottages in the villages were part of the Manor, with the many peasants working for the Lord of the Manor. It seems fitting, therefore, to devote most of this short village history to show how the poor people were unfairly treated by the King and his followers. Farming up to the 18th century was a very simple business, with many wooden implements still in use. Gradually, new ideas, improved machinery, and the better breeding methods of farm animals improved agriculture.

Unfortunately, there was a bad side to this situation. In Bagworth and Thornton there were large stretches of common land where the peasant farmers grazed their cows, pigs, etc. and grew simple crops. The King's henchmen found trumped-up excuses to seize this land and hand it over to their own hand-picked landowners. Parliament, being largely controlled by these landowners, passed laws legalising the seizure. Without this common land many villagers could no longer get a living in the countryside and had to seek work in the towns, emigrate or starve.

After the Norman Conquest in 1066, William I (The Conqueror) replaced the English Lords with his Norman (French) followers, giving to each the control of a number of villages which the Normans called 'Manors'.

William claimed all the land for himself — forest, field, marsh and moorland. His barons could own none: they merely held their 'Manors' for the King as his tenants. In return they had to fight for him and provide the Royal Household with a share of the Manor's produce.

William shocked everyone by sending his men to every Manor to enquire its size and to produce a detailed record of everything, including the number of peasants, animals, ploughs, mills, land, etc. This information was collected and by 1086 it was all written down in what is known as the 'Domesday Book'. The Barons and Bailiffs, in turn, expected the utmost service from their English peasants, consequently village or manorial life grew harder than ever.

From the **'LEICESTERSHIRE MEDIEVAL VILLAGE NOTES' by G.F. Farnham, Vol. V 1931,** and in the Victorian County History of Leicestershire 1. P.338 Domesday Survey about 1086 it states that the land of the men of the Count of Mellent. Ralph holds of the Court 9 Carucates of land in Bageworde. (One carucate was about 120 acres of land).

SO BAGWORTH EXISTED AT THE NORMAN CONQUEST!

In the **'MEDIEVAL PARKS OF LEICESTERSHIRE' by L.M. CANTOR,** he records that **Bagworth Park was in existence in 1279,** when it belonged to the Bishop of Durham. Almost a century later it had passed to Robert Holland, and by 1411 to Matilda Lovel.

Commoners Lose Out

It was probably disparked between 1411 and 1474. Later, Lord Hastings, Knight, was licenced by King Edward IV to impark 2,000 acres of land and wood with lime and stone. This park is shown on Saxton's map of 1576 and listed by Burton in 1641 as being 'now in use' with the manor house it contained being halfway between the two villages, and common to both.

In the **'DIRECTORY OF LEICESTER AND RUTLAND 1877' by William White,** it is quoted thus:

THORNTON Parish, which is in Market Bosworth Union & County Court District and Sparkenhoe Hundred, includes the townships of Bagworth, Stanton-under-Bardon & Thornton.

Its village is pleasantly situated on rising ground between two small rivulets on the east side of the Leicester to Burton railway & 9 miles west by north of Leicester.

BAGWORTH is a village, township & chapelry in Thornton Parish, 10 miles W.N.W. of Leicester, on the west side of the Leicester to Burton railway. It contains 505 inhabitants and about 2,141 acres of land forming a picturesque district of hill and dale, watered by several small rivulets. In the reign of Queen Elizabeth I (1558 - 1603), Henry Earl of Huntingdon, Lord Hastings, sold this manor and the Park to Sir James Harrington, knight, of Burley in Rutland.

FROM J. NICHOLS' HISTORY & ANTIQUITIES OF THE COUNTY OF LEICESTER, VOL IV, PART II: In 1609 Sir Henry Harrington, knight, seized the manor of Bagworth and 46 acres of land, and at his court held on **July 7th 1609** granted these tenements to ***EDWARD ORME, his wife FRANCES and WILLIAM ORME, son of the said EDWARD, for all his life. And it is the custom that every tenant has common pasture in Bagworth Heath containing 300 acres of pasture.***

The lordship of Bagworth was soon after sold by Sir Wm. Harrington (Sir James' grandson), to **Sir Robert Banaster, knight, Master of the Household to King James I.**

The Park and Manor was garrisoned by the army of Charles I during the Civil War with Cromwell (1642-1649), when it was devastated and disparked soon afterwards. It then belonged to Lady Frances Manners.

WHITE'S DIRECTORY (1877) tells us: in Bagworth Park, a farmhouse called *'THE MOATS'* is still surrounded by a dry moat, from which numerous deer horns and bones have been dug. Many spear and arrow heads, bullets and cannon balls have been found in the grounds.

In his **HISTORICAL SKETCH OF THORNTON, BAGWORTH AND STANTON, by Rev. Horace Cooper,** he states that in 1761 Thomas Brailsford exchanged the benefice and great tithes of Thornton and

Bagworth Park Farm – Original site of 'The Manor' and 'The Moats'. The dry moat can be seen to the right hand side of the farmhouse.

Bagworth with Lord Viscount Maynard's land in Botcheston, near Newtown Unthank. Thus, it came about that the influential Maynard family acquired land in this Parish — tapping rich coal reserves at Bagworth in 1825. He goes on to say that between 1779 and 1794 most of the common fields around Thornton and Bagworth were enclosed by Lord Maynard, the Duke of Rutland and Nicholas Grundy after an Act of Parliament was passed.

Near to the Manor is Bagworth Heath, two miles in length and one and a half miles in width. The part belonging to the Manor was enclosed in 1794 and in 1795 the open fields were also enclosed.

Thus we have unfolded the background which caused the underlying difficulties that were encountered by Baptists (or Nonconformists, as they were known) in purchasing ground on which to build a chapel in the parish. In 1796, when Samuel Deacon raised the Cross at Bagworth, **the big landowners, such as Lord Maynard, supported the established Anglican Church — Thornton St. Peter's, and Bagworth Holy Rood.** He also built the schools and gave financial support to scholars. That is why the Baptist Movement was not welcomed by many when it arrived in 1796, **and why their church was built in 'No-Man's-Land'.**

Old pen and ink sketch of St. Peter's, Thornton in 1792

Old pen and ink sketch of Holy Rood Bagworth

CHAPTER 2

THE BAPTISTS: . . . The Great Awakening!

To give our story of Cross Hills full credulity we must go right back to the early 18th century, to Wales, where the dawn of the 'Great Awakening' was about to take place. It was in 1735 that brave, dauntless men, like Griffith Jones, Howell Harris and Daniel Rowlands went out preaching a new style of worship. A style that breathed fresh life into religion at a time when Christian belief was faltering in the conventional church, and morale was at an all-time low. This was a time when the Church was prepared to go out to the people, instead of always the reverse. The preachers went forth and spread the Word with zeal and enthusiasm, out in the fields and meeting places, even before their own churches were built. This dawn of the Great Awakening was called the 'Evangelical Revival'

In England of that same year, a forerunner of this great revival was a man named George Whitefield. He had been converted along with names like John and Charles Wesley. Whitefield spread his new beliefs around the south of England with great vitality. In 1737 he teamed up with John Wesley, preaching to 30,000 converts in Bristol, then onwards to move the London crowds. In Kingswood, Bristol, 10,000 miners stood in the open air listening as one to the true gospel preaching of Whitefield.

Lady Selina, Countess of Huntingdon

Honoured as 'the greatest preacher England ever produced' Whitefield's charisma and energy spread the Word like wildfire, from the south up into the Midlands, and into Leicestershire's Charnwood Forest by the year 1740.

Lady Selina, Countess of Huntingdon, who lived at Donington Park, was sympathetic to Whitefield and the Wesleys' teachings and became converted by them. At this time the morale and

Christian teachings and beliefs were at a low ebb at every level of society, including the established Church. No Sunday schools existed to educate our children in religion, and few people could read the very scarce Christian literature available.

Lady Selina was born at Staunton Harold in 1707 and died in London in 1791 aged 84 years. She became a devout and strong Christian, making Whitefield one of her Chaplains. She invited aristocracy, the wealthy and important people of society to her home to hear him preach the Word. During her lifetime she built many chapels and schools, in which she installed vigorous evangelical preachers of the highest calibre. She became known as 'The Patroness of the Revival', and wherever resistance barred the way by way of ridicule, contempt and mockery, her domestic chapels and private rooms supplied the necessary meeting places. During her life, much of Selina's private wealth was expended building Sunday schools, meeting houses and chapels around the country, bringing the gospel within the grasp of aristocracy and the poor alike.

When resistance to the evangelical tidal wave affected parliament, a new law was brought out in 1779 compelling the registration of her chapels as 'Non-conformist meeting houses'. They became known as the 'Countess of Huntingdon Connexion', and the name stuck permanently.

The Wesley brothers, John and Charles, were synonymously linked with Whitefield during the great revival. Whitefield was appointed as one of Lady Selina's chaplains, preaching to her wealthy and influential friends twice a week at her home at Donington Park.

John Wesley, also having close connections with Lady Selina, went to preach at Melbourne and Markfield in 1741, where she owned property. A few days later a loyal servant of the Countess, David Taylor, went out with her blessing and preached in Glenfield and Ratby. This proved to be a crucial meeting, a great cross roads for the Midlands, because at this meeting Samuel Deacon senior was present and he was awakened to serve the Lord.

A more complete history of the Deacon family is covered in chapter four. Below, the Deacons are mentioned to place them in the general situation of the story.

Samuel Deacon senior, a former farm labourer who lived to the great age of 98 (1714 - 1812) had recently settled into his new home in Ratby. At the time that David Taylor's preaching reached him, Deacon was a bell ringer in the established Anglican church. The manner of his conversion was dramatic: he was mowing in the fields, scything the grass, when he laid down his implement to hear Taylor's message of the Lord. Becoming thoroughly awakened by the sermon, Samuel saw fit to take the extreme action of leaving the Anglican church, setting up as an evangelical preacher and pastor in Ratby.

Often his work called on him to walk a round distance of 40 or 50 miles, summer and winter, in order to preach in several villages. Three services were frequently held on Sundays, requiring long hours and the constitution of an ox. He would walk from Ratby to Melbourne, a distance of 20 miles, perform a hard day's preaching and arrive home deep into the early hours. All this on top of his work as a grocer in Ratby, when he would often need to carry goods all the way from Leicester on his back!

In 1782 Deacon moved to Barton in the Beans, aged 68, and was to continue his evangelistic preaching well into his 80's. When he died in 1812 he was buried in the chapel there, a rare privilege usually reserved only for ministers. Samuel Deacon senior richly deserved this honour, having been a pastor for 52 years and a preacher for 60 years.

As Whitefield and Wesley had discovered elsewhere, the new style of preaching in 1741 had not initially been welcomed at Barton. John Whyatt's home, amongst others, was vandalized; they tried to drown other prominent preachers, such as John Aldridge, and an assault on Joseph Donisthorpe was almost fatal. Others had their clothes torn, pelted with turf and dung and dragged through filth. They blackened John Taylor's face, cut his clothes and scalped his hair. Consequently, the persecution of the evangelical preachers and their followers became so bad that meetings had to be conducted in private for a time.

Mr Samuel Deacon I, (snr.) among the first Pastors of Barton church (Dec 3rd 1714 - Mar 19th 1812)

John Taylor of Markfield — not to be confused with David Taylor — preached at Osbaston at a villager's request, and was attended by people from Barlestone, Newbold Verdon, Cadeby and Nailstone. He so impressed John Whyatt of Barton in the Beans, and later John Aldridge, that they invited Taylor to Barton where he preached in John Whyatt's house.

It was in 1743, two years after the first sermon that they decided to form a body of church believers called the Barton Society. It consisted of seven members: John Whyatt, John Aldridge, William Adcock, Stephen Dixon, William and Mrs Kendrick, and the groups good friend, David Taylor.

The first small chapel was built in the centre of Barton in 1745 at a cost of £170. It was of two Storeys, the upstairs used for accommodating unmarried male and female members. They adopted the name of 'Independents' until in 1755 they decided to become 'Baptists'. By 1760 Barton could not cope with the rapid growth, being the centre of an of Baptist followers. It soon became necessary to set up five independent churches in and around Melbourne.

The Barton church was now well and truly established, having a proper, if small, building in which to worship. In 1755 a major change developed in their sentiments and practice with regard to the ordinance of baptism. At first, infants were sprinkled with water; later they were immersed in a large tub placed inside the church.

The Baptists were soon after compelled to acknowledge that by virtue of the authority of the New Testament, dipping infants was not acceptable and they should only be sprinkled with water. From then on, only 'believers' were fully immersed. After much deliberation, Mr Donisthorpe baptised Mr Kendrick, then Mr Kendrick baptised Mr Donisthorpe. Then united in their mission, they went out and baptised 60 or 70 followers, continuing with considerable success.

Then one day in 1760, an injurious incident took place, whereby Mr Kendrick had charges brought against him which resulted in his ultimate exclusion from the fellowship. Reports suggested that for some time, Mr Kendrick had desired too great a power, one of the charges being that he artfully secured possession of the deeds of several meeting houses. The only way he could be persuaded to hand back the legal documents was by the exchange of money in his favour.

As provision for a baptistry large enough for adults was not available inside Barton church, it had to be constructed outside in the grounds. The remains are still there to be seen today.

The original Barton chapel, after its construction in 1745, was enlarged in 1801 and again in 1809. But from the Records Office, Wigston Magna, it was possible to establish that several such enlargements took place. The following is an extract from an original letter seen in the Leicestershire Records Office: '... the meeting house at Barton has been enlarged six times in the last 30 years of Samuel Deacon's ministry'.

But still the chapel building outgrew its congregations and by 1840 it was finally demolished to make way for a more spacious church. It was officially opened a year later and is still the current building.

Under the Barton Church, from 1760 preaching spread to groups of devoted followers in Hugglescote, Ibstock, Whitwick, Stanton-under-Bardon and Hinckley. Others followed, with churches at Barlestone (1779); Market Bosworth (1774); Bagworth (1814); Measham (1811); Congerstone (1821); Newbold Verdon (1831); Desford (1861).

Samuel Deacon, Junior, (let us call him Samuel Deacon II for clarities sake throughout this publication) was born in Ratby in 1746, one year after the building of Barton's first church. He started off as a farm labourer in service in Melbourne. Not given to farming, he began to develop his own inventive flare of mechanical devices. Soon, influential people began to take notice, and he was able to secure a clock-making apprenticeship at the age of 16 with Joseph Donisthorpe of Normanton-le-Heath.

Joseph also ran a blacksmith's business, and had come under the strong influence of David Taylor's preaching. He spoke freely of his new beliefs to the many farmers who brought their horses to the forge. A good number were often persuaded to stay for upwards of three hours to listen to his delivery of the gospel. When Donisthorpe moved to Loughborough in 1766, Samuel Deacon still had much to learn about clockmaking. He was yet but 20 years old, and he decided to move to the town with his master to further his career.

At the age of 21 Samuel pronounced his belief in Christ and was baptised. During his employment at Loughborough, he walked many times to Barton church to worship, then back home on a circular route that encompassed Leicester.

Donisthorpe became the first pastor of the Loughborough General Baptist Church and loved his work so much that he declared he wished to die preaching. In May, 1774, his wish was granted when he collapsed and expired in the pulpit.

In 1777 Deacon junior, aged 31, married the daughter of William Adcock, one of the original seven founders of Barton church. Deacon moved to Barton that year, started his own highly successful clock-making business and preached his first service on August 1st. Barely twenty months later, when the bluebells carpeted the woods, Samuel was appointed pastor at Barton and joined his father in a unique partnership.

In addition to preaching all round the district in his new capacity of pastor, Samuel junior developed his unique clock making business, the quality of which was set to be renowned far and wide. But his talents did not stop there: he also helped establish Baptist churches up and down the western flank of Leicestershire.

The first Barton chapel was built in 1745, cost £170 and measured just 36 ft by 22 ft.

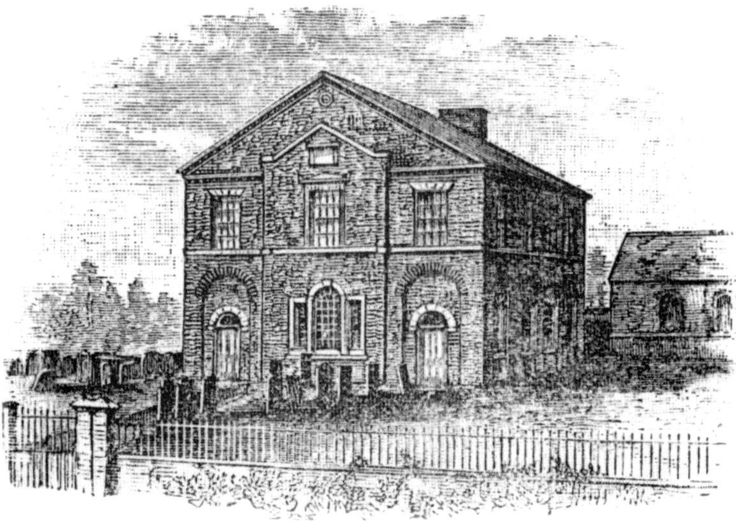

A new, grander chapel was constructed in 1841 at a cost of £900. This chapel still exists and is in regular use today

CHAPTER 3

FORMATION OF THE NEW CONNEXION OF GENERAL BAPTISTS

An important phase in the Evangelical Revival should be mentioned here. On June 7th, 1770, 24 men assembled in a plain brick meeting house at the rear of Whitechapel church, London. Only two of the men were from the Capital, 19 were preachers, and all were members or pastors delegated by their churches to form a new religious community. Of the 24, only 10 steadfastly followed the new bond of the union, and of the 10, Samuel Deacon senior, from Barton in the Beans was the eldest. Also from Leicestershire were three others: John Grimley, of Loughborough; John Tarratt, of Kegworth; and Nathaniel Pickering of Castle Donington.

Mr Samuel Deacon II, (jnr.)
Clockmaker

A preliminary hearing had taken place at Lincoln nine months earlier, in a quaint old chapel under the shadow of the City's magnificent cathedral. A resolution was passed to come together at Whitechapel, in London, which they were now doing. All were looked down upon by so-called members of the orthodox church, who classed them as Dissenters, Independents, Congregationalists, or Nonconformists. It all depended on what took their fancy; the whim of the day! By the study of the Bible the new preachers became Baptists, although outsiders named them **Protestant Dissenters.**

Although the new faith had existed for quite a few years, there had been no formal formation or naming. On June 7th, 1770, this situation changed when, at the assembly in Whitechapel, London, the **Independents became known as the New Connexion of General Baptists.**

In 1796 Samuel Deacon II began preaching in Whitwick, in the Division of Hugglescote. In the same year he brought the Gospel to Bagworth, which was soon to be extended to Thornton. A standard of the Cross was raised by Samuel II in Bagworth in 1796 to mark the arrival of the Baptists.

Among the numerous Baptist churches that sprang up in the late 18th century and early 19th century, was a certain little meeting house between Bagworth and Thornton. Built just off a sloping road, on a bend, travellers who were strange to the district would come across the church unexpectedly. The little church was built in no-man's-land, tucked well away from the sight of the established Anglican Churches of St. Peter, high in the village of Thornton, or Holy Rood, sitting aloft in the opposite direction at Bagworth. This little place of worship was built in 1814 and became known as Cross Hills Baptist Church. Previous to this, there had been eighteen years of struggle and strife, persecution and prejudice, inflicted by so-called members of the established church. There had been the acute difficulty of finding a landowner brave or willing enough to sell the nonconformists a piece of suitable building land to erect a permanent home.

Meetings were held out in the open air at first and then in cottages. Mr. Thomas Smith threw open his Bagworth abode as a meeting place and on September 13th 1800 his house was licensed for preaching. Thus, meetings of the Baptists continued until a small piece of ground could be purchased, clearing the way for the erection of a permanent building by 1814. This original Cross Hills church site is still the location of the modern version today.

This letter, or report, on the poor state of the Barton Church was obtained from Leics. Records Office. We do not know to whom it was sent, as it was addressed 'Dear Sir', neither was it signed, but it was written from Barton on November 20th 1814.

Since Aug: 4 – 1798 we have baptized about ~~200~~ two hundred and ~~eigh~~ eighty. We have lost about fifty by death. Have put away about forty six. Several have removed to other churches: We have now about three hundred members, many of whom are very poor.

We are now in a desolate state. Our aged Pastor. Mr Samuel Deacon; died March 19th 1812, in the 98 year of his age. The present Mr Saml Deacon, is in his 69th year, and so infirm, ~~that~~ he can preach but little, and has quite resigned the pastoral Office. Mr J: Brewin is very unwell, and has preached but seldom this ~~little the~~ present year; and we fear he is not likely to recover his ~~former~~ health. Mr ~~Harrison~~ ~~Hatsley~~ is well approved, but his health is so indifferent, that our hopes are greatly eclipsed. We have looked out, for years, to find a suitable person to serve us, but hitherto in vain. We have several respectable friends who can speak decently, but we sadly want a good Shepherd.

We have been at considerable expense, on many accounts, for ourselves and others. We first built a Meeting house at Barlestone at about 160 £ — Afterwards we had it to enlarge & to erect galleries &c. at about 150 £ expense. Barton Meetinghouse was old and decay'd and too small — That and the School-Rooms cost us about 400 £. We have *
* since built one near Bagworth, at upwards of 300 £. Beside what comes upon us daily, which would be tedious to mention.

We have lost, buried, many of our friends; and some of our best; whose names, we trust, are in the Book of Life; but whose names would not greatly adorn the page of History. We have had few of splendid abilities, or of unexampled piety, but many sincere christians. Such as Mr. Deacon, our late aged Pastor, who was remarkable for his knowledge of Scripture, uprightness, industry, economy, constancy, perseverance, and cheap travelling on foot, to the shame of many young and modern preachers. He died Mar: 19. 1812, ~~aged 94~~. We suppose he never kept his bed a day, till the day he died.

Mr. Thos. Webster our late Deacon 35 years, was a man of such eminence in his business, steadiness in the faith, integrity in his conduct, punctuality in his office, and strict honesty through life, ~~that~~ gaind him a high degree of reputation. He died suddenly, Dec: 17-1812. aged upwards of 70. He was a strong believer! being asked a few days before his death, how he was, he answerd, "pretty well! I cannot doubt! Thou wilt keep him in perfect peace whose heart is staid on thee because trusteth in thee. And I find it true, said he." It is worthy of notice that our Deacon, Mr Adcock, died suddenly, Jan: 19. 1808. much like his colegue in Office, Mr Webster. Both of them were of long standing in the same office, and of high repute in the church. Mr Adcock was one, and the last, of the first seven who joined in fellowship, and constituted the beginning of the new Connection.

We have about 300 members, and not one ordained person, save Mr J. Deacon who has resigned his office, and is obliged to rest from his labours.

Barton near Mt Bosworth
Leicestershire Nov: 20 - 1814

The Importance of Samuel

Whenever the name Samuel Deacon is mentioned in Leicestershire, or indeed, much farther afield, the mind springs automatically to 'movement'. By that we mean either to a clock movement or to the Baptist Movement. The Deacon family is synonymously and irrevocably linked to both. Therefore it would be irresponsible not to give the Deacons a chapter to highlight their special skills and talents.

Barton in the Beans is the 'capital' of the Baptist Movement in the area, from where it all originated, and it so happens that Cross Hills is on the very doorstep of Barton; only three miles away. That is where the Deacons settled and spread the Gospel many miles around them, where Deacon II made his mark as a renowned clock and watchmaker. Some of his valuable timepieces are working perfectly to this day, in stately homes, in museums and in antique shops around the country.

So let us indulge in a condensed family history of the unique lives of the Deacon family, who were inextricably connected with the mother church of Barton and had consequential influence on the formation of Cross Hills chapel.

CHAPTER 4

THE DEACON FAMILY OF LEICESTERSHIRE

The earliest record of the Deacon family in Leicestershire is that of John Deacon, soldier and farm labourer. John was the father of Samuel Deacon I, also often referred to as Samuel Deacon the aged, or Senior. Samuel Deacon I was the father of the clockmaker, Samuel Deacon II (or S. D. junior).

As a young man John Deacon fought under William III in 1690 at the Battle of the Boyne, when James II was sent scuttling back to France. Upon his discharge, he made his home in Normanton-le-Heath near Ashby-de-la-Zouch in NW Leicestershire. Here he became farm labourer, a Church Warden and Clerk to the Parish. John was a family man, becoming father to four sons and three daughters. It was on March 20th 1722 that he finally expired and was buried in the village at Normanton.

Samuel Deacon I was the first of John's four sons, and lived to the grand age of 98 years. With the money he saved, Samuel I settled in Ratby in 1741, was married the following year and had three children: Elizabeth, Samuel II and William. Samuel II's elder sister and younger brother died in their infancy, he alone surviving to eventually become the famous clock-maker at Barton.

In 1782 Samuel Deacon I moved to Barton and rented a cottage from his clockmaker son at £2 per year. Being a shrewd businessman Samuel the elder became the landlord of four houses at Ratby from 1806, charging a rental of £8 per annum.

The first wife of Samuel I died in 1750. He remarried in 1755 to Mary Redburn and had three more children, John, Ann and Elizabeth. John, who grew up to learn clockmaking from his half brother Samuel II, became Minister of Friar Lane Baptists, in Leicester, and died in 1821. Another cruel blow was struck in 1762, when Samuel I became a widower for the second time. He remarried his third wife Sarah Stevenson in 1763, a lady described as 'advanced in years', and this time they were not blessed with children.

His son, Samuel Deacon II, was born at Ratby on February 2nd 1746 and was unfortunate to be only four years old when his mother died. This had dire repercussions for him as, in those days, schools were virtually non-existent. Basic education was administered by mothers to their children the best way they could. With the passing on of his mother, Samuel II's sparse primary education was confined to a few occasional reading lessons from an unnamed old woman. When he eventually left the village to enter farm work he soon found he was unable to read a single Chapter in the New Testament.

The reader should be aware that there were two clockmaking Samuel Deacons' whose careers overlapped. This lesser known clockmaker was a cousin (1771-1860), to whom Samuel Deacon II (1746-1816) fully expounded the art of clockmaking during the time the younger man was an apprentice and journeyman. As a result of this, confusion has sometimes been experienced among clock owners and buyers as to which Samuel Deacon was the maker of a particular time piece.

In 1805 Samuel Deacon II handed over the business to his cousin and namesake. Henceforth, in his 'retirement' at the age of 59, Samuel Deacon II continued to make clock movements for his cousin, although he now defined his trade as a watchmaker.

In Samuel II's early boyhood, as was the practice in those days, he left home to begin his working life, living in with his various employers. At the tender age of 11 he entered farm service at Melbourne, but was soon to be employed at East Leake, South Nottinghamshire. After a while Samuel II progressed to a Mr. Aldridge in Hertfordshire, where his career was to take a new twist.

Under Mr. Aldridge, Samuel's fortunes were eventually to change for the better, but not before suffering many lashings by whip and halter (as was the usual procedure in the training of young employees) for the lack of interest he showed in farmwork. Instead of concentrating on carts, ploughs and fertilisers, young Samuel's flair for mechanical contrivances was desperately trying to manifest itself.

In the fields in which he laboured, he would gouge a circular furrow in the earth, plunging a vertical stick into the centre. By observing the moving shadow thrown by the stick, Samuel could tell the hour of the day, thus creating his first primitive clock in the form of a sundial.

The ingenuity of Samuel became further apparent on the occasion when a travelling acquaintance of Mr. Aldridge broke his journey, to lodge overnight at the farm. The traveller, it seemed, had the need for a pair of nutcrackers, and Samuel II promptly produced one of his own gadgets made earlier from wood. Upon inspection, the craftsmanship of the nutcrackers so impressed the traveller that he was later compelled to share the details of it with a clockmaker in Normanton-le-Heath. A letter to Mr. Aldridge came back from Joseph Donisthorpe, offering a bound apprenticeship in the sum of £12 to Samuel Deacon II at the age of sixteen in the year 1762. This marked the end of Samuel II's relatively short farming career and the dawning of his true vocation: that of a clockmaker.

Donisthorpe taught Deacon II only certain clockmaking techniques that brought in his immediate income. The real theory and skills of the trade were denied the young pupil, and Samuel was pleased when his apprenticeship ended in 1768. Fortunately, due to Samuel's own avid interest and application, he had virtually self taught himself how to forge, file, engrave and turn on the lathe to a level of efficiency better than most craftsmen. After leaving Joseph Donisthorpe, Samuel joined clockmaker Thomas Lindley at his Leicester business. Samuel rented rooms in Union Street where he was later joined by his half brother, John Deacon, who attended a Leicester school. It was at these premises, in his spare time, that Samuel made some clocks by his own initiative, simultaneously teaching John the art of clockmaking in the process.

Above: A Joseph Donisthorpe long case clock – now in the Newarke Museum.

While working for Lindley, Samuel met, and came under guidance of, a brilliant clockmaker, mathematician and mechanical genius by the name of Rev. William Ludlam. Under his wing Samuel Deacon II learned the belated theory of clockmaking and much more. Ludlam spent much time with his eager pupil, showing him how to make chime and musical clocks and presenting him with relevant coloured drawings.

Below: Notice in Samuel Deacon II workshop at Leicester Newark House Museum

DEACON

WATCH & CLOCKMAKER

JEWELLER ETC.

REGISTRAR OF MARRIAGES

Deacon II was a very methodical man, keeping records concerning much of his clockmaking life. He kept many notebooks, one of his earliest registering that he first became a journeyman (a skilled clockmaker) in 1768 on completion of his apprenticeship. He also saw fit to note in 1769 that for sustenance he began to eat a loaf of bread, costing him one penny, a slab of cheese 6d and 1 pint of ale which was 1$^{1}/_{2}$d.

1771 was a very significant year for Samuel II, moving to Barton-in-the-Beans to start his own clockmaking business. He was married to william Adcock's daughter, Elizabeth, paying his father-in-law £3 per annum to set up home and workshop on the premises. This seemed an idyllic business setup as Adcock, being a carpenter, made the clock cases for Samuel at between £1 and £1-5s-0d each.

It is thought, from receipts for building materials, that in 1796 Samuel II extended the premises as the business flourished. Samuel made all the tools for his workshop, his lathe taking five days to make, according to his records. He even made — and used — dentists tools, as are on display at Newarke Houses Museum, Leicester, in his actual reconstructed workshop there.

As a matter of interest John Verow, who was an apprentice & Journeyman of Samuel Deacon, set up his own clockmaking business in Barton Fabis, working in opposition to his former master until 1795.

From an early age Samuel II suffered ill health, particularly from gall stones. In his last five years on earth his health considerably deteriorated, and on March 2nd 1816, aged 70, he died of a stroke. As was the privilege for ministers, Samuel II joined his father, being buried inside Barton chapel.

An impression of Samuel Deacon's workshop at Barton Fabis, built up from old photographs and painted by Mr David Cowley, of Hinckley, Leics.

In the second half of the 18th century the Leicestershire clockmaking industry was largely dominated by one man – Samuel Deacon II. He was born at Ratby in 1746 and as a boy was apprenticed to clockmaker Joseph Donisthorpe of Normanton-le-Heath. In 1771 Samuel Deacon set up his own workshop at Barton-in-the-Beans, near Market Bosworth. He was a skilled craftsman and jeweller. He made timepieces of every type, from verge watches to turret clocks. He also made his own tools, including the lathe and wheel-cutting machine and undertook his own forging and casting. Samuel Deacon was a deeply religious man and was a deacon at the Baptist church. When he died at the age of 70 in 1816 the business passed to his son John.

Exterior of the Deacon workshop in Barton Fabis showing left, Mr John Daniell; far right, Mr T.W. Deacon

It was in 1951 that Mr John Daniell, then Assistant Keeper of Antiquities at this Museum, heard that the last of the male line of Deacons - Mr T. W. Deacon - had decided to sell the family home and workshop. On the chance that there might still be some old tools left, he investigated. To his amazement he found Samuel Deacon's original workshop of 1771 virtually intact. The wheel cutting machine, the wooden horse to test clock movements, part of the lathe were all still there. The workbench was littered with tools and cabinets. Later Deacons had added to it, and there were also later movements and dials. Up in the roof space, under the dust and rubbish of more than a century, were Samuel Deacon's account books, workshop records and material relating to the Baptist church (all now kept at the Leicestershire Record Office). The complete contents of the workshop were removed to the museum. At first it was housed in an 18th century workshop in Castle View, Leicester, but in 1983 it was reassembled in this room. It is believed to be one of the earliest surviving clockmaker's workshops in this country.

Displayed in the Newarke Museum, Leicester

The Samuel Deacon clock with 'Biblical Scene'

The photograph shows Samuel Deacon's clock which had the 'Biblical Scene' painted at the top of the white oval dial. The clock was believed to have been made for Sir Wolstan Dixie, of Market Bosworth. Note the picture on the face of the clock showing the angel stopping Abraham from sacrificing Isaac, his son, and the ram caught in the thicket.

An even more remarkable timepiece was the Samuel Deacon 'Masterpiece' longcase clock, made in 1790. This clock played sixty-five tunes on nineteen bells and wires, and had four chime barrels. The clock was made for the Rev. William Severn, of Hinckley. Having a case of solid mahogany, the upper section of the white face exhibited a band of musicians. While the clock played a tune, three figures beat exact time to the music and three played on their instruments. At the same time a boy and girl danced in time to the music. The musical works was called a 'Lyricord' and would play either fortissimo or pianissimo, *(Loud or Quiet).*

Deacon's own description of his masterpiece, written in his records: '*... on the whole, without exaggeration, it may be considered the completest piece of clockwork ever exhibited in these parts.*'

The clock appeared in the sale of the contents of Cossington Lodge, Leicestershire, on September 14th 1868, and is thought not to have realised a great deal of money. In March 1970 the clock was again sold in auction.

The Deacon workshop – reconstructed in the Newarke Museum, Leicester

Barton Fabis Baptist Sunday School - Centenary Memorial, 1900.

Left: Mr. John Derry – Pastor from 1824 - 1852. This portrait hangs in the Barton Chapel.

Below: Barton Chapel – in the rain

PART II: THE FIRST CROSS HILLS BAPTIST CHAPEL

CHAPTER 5

BAPTIST CHAPEL – in 'NO MAN'S LAND'

This is the story of succeeding Cross Hills Baptist Church buildings that have been erected on the same spot between Thornton and Bagworth since the 19th century. There have been three buildings; the first was constructed in 1814, the second church was built in 1885 and the present church erected in 1996.

A law was passed in 1779 that made it necessary to register all non-conformist churches separately. An air of doubt and suspicion pervaded among many members of the Church of England, who frowned upon these 'upstart' General Baptists. There are many accounts of Baptists being attacked, robbed and their property broken into by thugs who classed themselves as supporters of the Anglican Church.

Eighteen years went by before land could be purchased (1796 - 1814), from the time when Deacon first raised the Standard of the Cross in Bagworth, until the Baptist church was first built at Cross Hills. These pioneers found they had to build in 'No Man's Land', between the two villages.

Countess of Warwick Daughter of Viscount Maynard

At the time the first Cross Hills church was erected, much of the land around the parish of Bagworth and Thornton was owned by Viscount Maynard, who later sunk the shafts of Bagworth colliery on his estate in 1825. Frances Evelyn Maynard (Daisy, as she was known) inherited this land and the hugely profitable mineral rights in 1865 at the age of four. She also inherited estates in Essex where she went to live with her mother and sister. In 1880, five years before the second Cross Hills church was built, she married the Earl of Warwick, to become Countess.

So Cross Hills church had to be erected on neutral ground, on a small plateau cut into the hillside, across the road from nearby Bagworth Park. The road runs down at a gradient from the two villages, and about three quarters of the way down from Bagworth is the cut-out for the church and the graveyard. A stranger motoring down the hill and wanting to reach the church could easily overshoot the site, being also on a bend, warranting a drivers full attention.

In 1797 Jacob Brewin was appointed Assistant Minister of the Church at Barton in the Beans, having in his charge branches at Barlestone and Bagworth. This was years before Cross Hills was actually built, the branch congregating in meeting houses prior to having a church. Jacob Brewin was credited with playing a vital role in the founding of the first Cross Hills Chapel.

Like many of the non-conformist preachers, Brewin endured his own share of suffering and poverty. In 1800 a letter was circulated among the congregations that Mr Brewin had been dismissed from his live-in service with a Mr Astley, leaving Jacob without a roof over his head. Preaching the gospel, was given as the root reason for his dismissal from service. The Baptist Church, feeling responsible for Mr Brewin's well-being, stepped in.

Robert Hall, M.A. preached at the opening of the 1814 chapel.

A scheme was adopted by the Mother Church at Barton to erect a house in half an acre of ground in Barlestone. Mr Brewin would be installed in the house for the duration of his official capacity for the church, after which it would become the home of the current Minister or Pastor. The total cost of site and building was to be upwards of £150, of which £50 was already available. This was to be initially funded by Samuel Deacon, who then would seek to retrieve his

This copy of a letter, also obtained from Leics. Records Office, describes how Mr. Jacob Brewin was sacked and made homeless – because he dared to preach. How the Baptist Church responded by buying half an acre of ground at Barlestone on which they erected a house where he could live, and which would subsequently house succeeding ministers.

A few Observations concerning the dwelling house at Barlestone Jan'y. 1800.

It is well known by most of us, that some time ago Mr. Brewin was dismissed from the service of Mr. Astley, and discharged from his house; and thereby put into a situation very destressing. And as it was pretty evedent, that he suffered this through belonging to us, and preaching the Gospel; it was thought right that we should exert ourselves to provide him a dwelling. Accordingly about half an acre of ground was purchased at Barlestone, and a house erected thereon, in which Mr. Brewin now lives. The whole expence will amount to upwards of 150£. Towards this there is about 50£ already subscribed, as the following statement will show. Consequently Mr. D. who is the sole agent in this affair, is a great deal of money out of pocket. As things are thus circumstanced, we are come by the advice of the Church to solicit you to contribute according to your

(1)

ability to this act of Charity.

You will observe, that whatever you contribute, will be the property of the Church at Barton, and that Mr. Brewin will enjoy the advantage of it while the Church continue him in his present Office or capacity. That after him, it will be applyed to another in his place, or to the Minister or Pastor. So that the more we exert ourselves now, the less we shall have to do hereafter. It may be also proper to remark, this is to the Cause of Jesus Christ, and we hope it may be of use to posterity for generations yet unborn: and what we do for the Lord, he will undoubtedly repay with an abundant increace, either in this World or another.

If it be not convenient to pay the money now, a signification of what you propose will suffice; the money may be communicated when convenient, either together or in parts. &c.

The Lord loves a cheerful giver.

(2)

outlay through a regular subscription system. This scheme was widely adopted by the Barton church, as illustrated by an extract from Samuel Deacon's May 1827 receipt book for Bagworth and Thornton.

Very little is known about the 1814 chapel, or these 'meeting rooms', as they were then called. We have no illustrations to go on; no drawings or plans. From information passed on from our ancestors it is almost certain to have been a 'single storey' building, with facilities for a Sunday school. In extracts from a letter stored in the archives of the Records Office in Wigston Magna, Leicestershire, and written on November 20th, 1814, '...since August 4th, 1798, we have baptised 280. We are now in a poor state since Samuel Deacon died in 1812. ...we have since built one meeting house near Bagworth at upwards of £300.' (See page 15)

So we know that the first Cross Hills chapel cost around £300 to build in 1814.

From the very first time it was decided to build the 1814 Cross Hills Chapel, money and finance was a constant problem for its members. We read that the Standard was first raised by Samuel Deacon, junior, in 1796, and yet the first chapel was not built until 18 years later. Also, we know of many problems encountered in acquiring a suitable plot of land at that time, largely through prejudice from the orthodox Church.

Money was very scarce in 1796. But the building land had to be paid for somehow, and then came the cost of the chapel itself. Our ancestors had to save up a lot longer than 18 years to purchase what was required— at

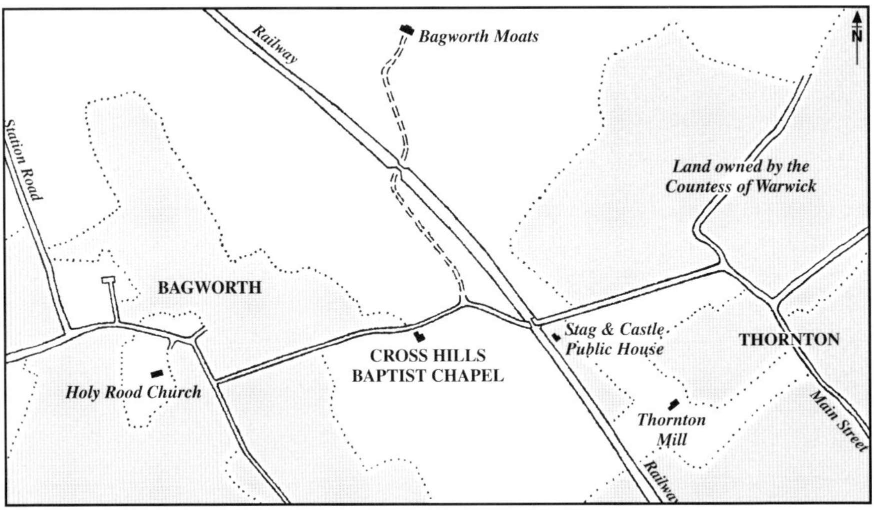

Plan (not to scale) showing position of Cross Hills Baptist chapel and land owned by the Countess of Warwick in 1919.

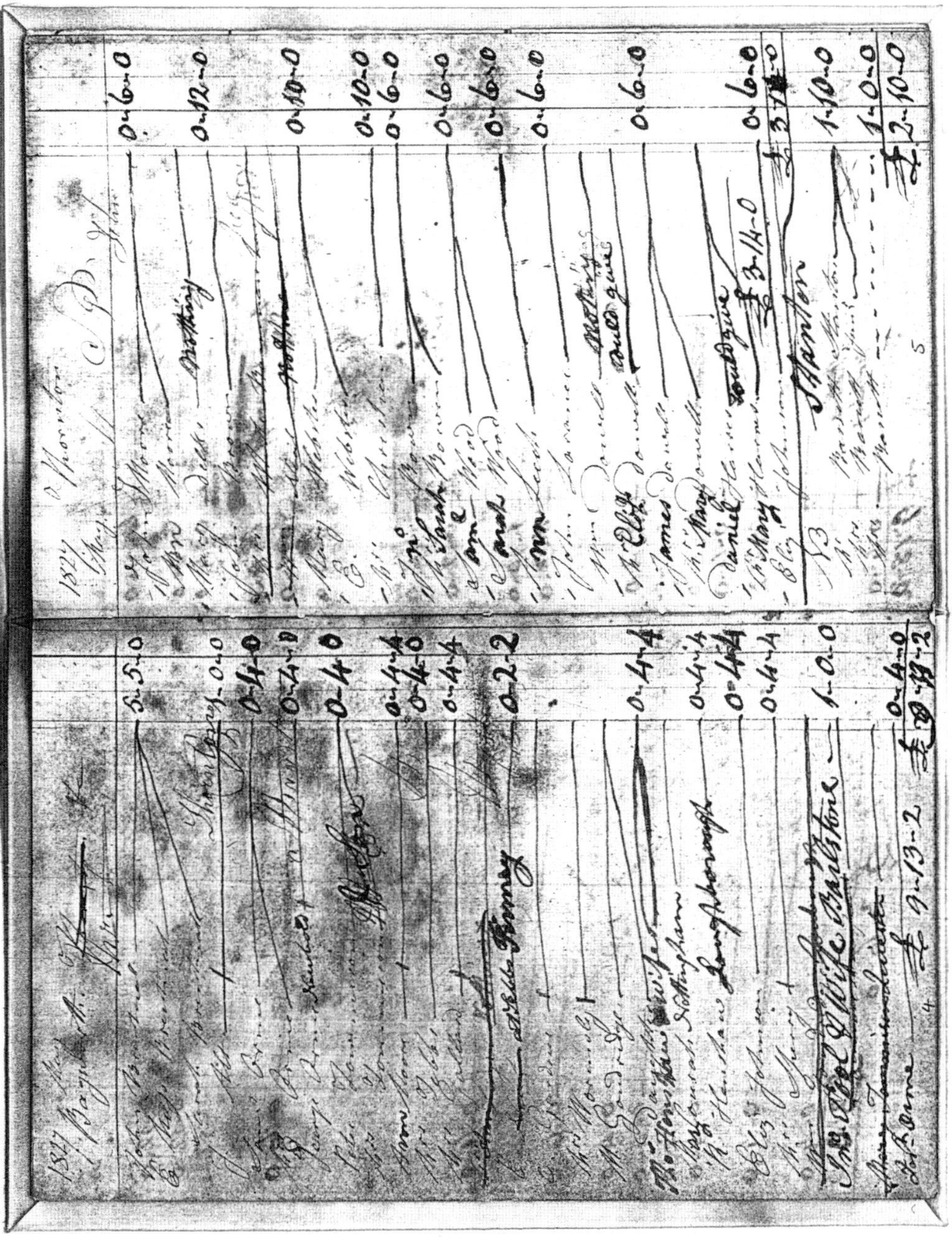

A section of subscription book, showing list of subscribers for Bagworth & Thornton, May 1827. The record was probably kept by Samuel Deacon's successors.
Note: 'nothing – could give' is written where members have not responded.

the right price and in a suitable venue. Even in 1827 the amount still owing on Cross Hills was £22-0s-0d, a great deal of money in those days.

Foundation stones of the oldest original chapel (1814) were found to be still in place, undisturbed, when the 1885 building was pulled down in 1995. Excavation work uncovered them running parallel to the road. The 1814 construction stood at right angles to the 1885 chapel. Also, the first chapel was built with the altar nearest Bagworth and the main entrance doors nearest Thornton, according to living memory.

A plot of land measuring 17 yards by 17 yards was the original site on which stood the 1814 chapel. The line of green slate foundation stones was almost certain to be the side of the chapel nearest the road. On the plan can be seen marked the location of the stones in their approximate position. (See page 49)

Note: The dark green foundation stones of the original 1814 chapel may be seen today, incorporated in the new Memorial Garden.

It is noted that alterations took place from time to time. In 1857 'new schools were erected at Cross Hills. School rooms were attached, and the chapel was reseated'.

It has been expressed that little evidence exists on the running of the 1814 chapel, as no minutes of meetings are available. **However, an account record book giving detailed income and expense does exist covering the years 1859 - 1947,** which reveals quite a lot regarding the buildings and the people who ran the church during this period.

For example, in 1861 most of the income generated for the children was donated for purchasing such things as hymn books and writing books in the Sunday school. Expense sheets recorded the buying of hymn books, bibles— which were 2/6d each, candles for church lighting, coals for the stove and Brunswick black lead at 1/- a bottle for cleaning it. The chapel cleaner, Mrs. Marvin, was paid £1-10-0d per year.

Some of the entries in these early account record books leave room for speculation as to their exact meaning. At the time of publication the authors leave some of the queries still to be answered or verified, and would be grateful for any help regarding the unusual entries.

On October 12th 1861 this strange entry was recorded: 'Bow belonging the bass new haired— 1/6d'.

This 'bass' seemed to cause a lot of trouble in maintenance, as it is documented as having to be transported and repaired regularly though the years. Written in the back of the book in 1861 is a subscription list for the purchase of this 'bass'.

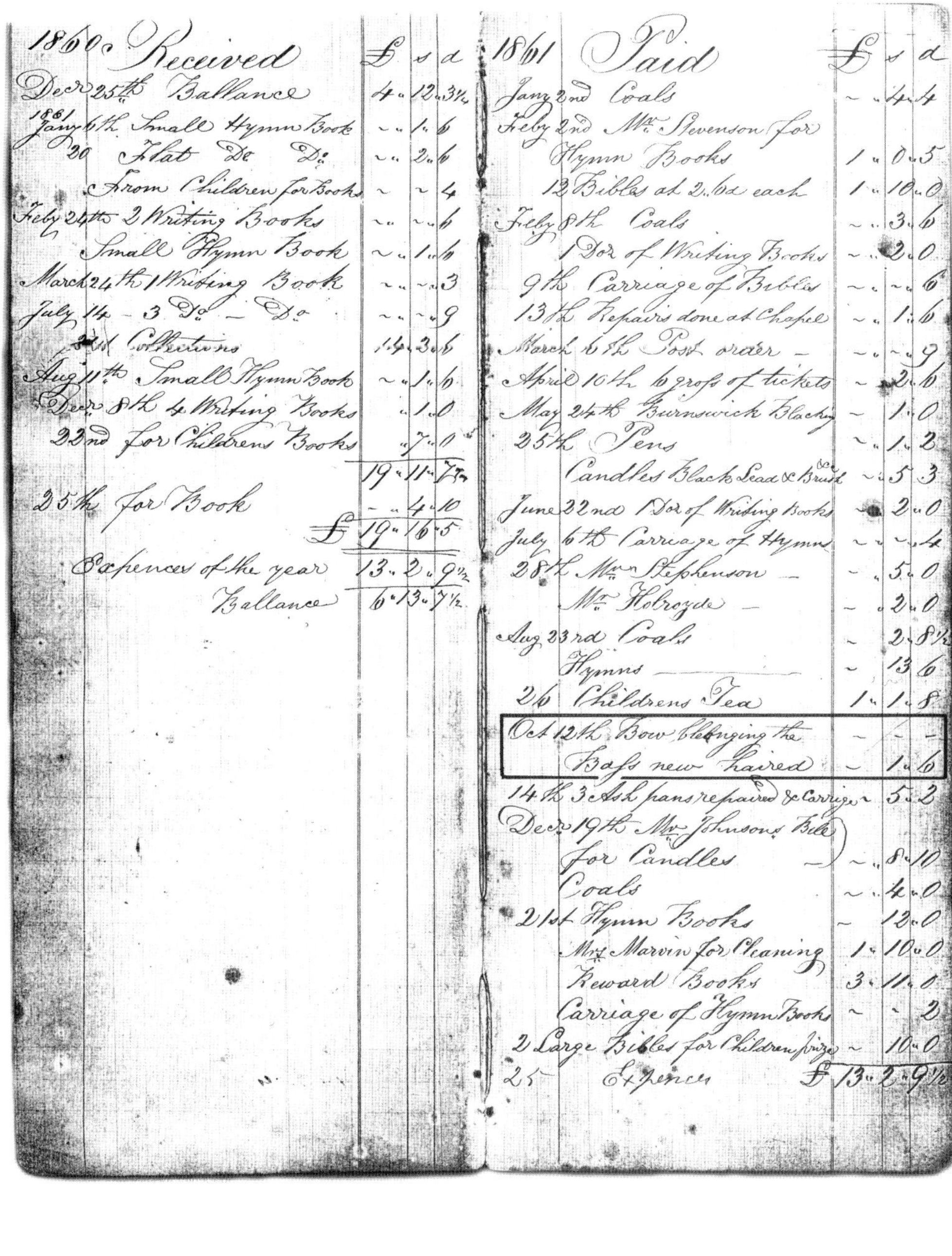

1860 Received	£	s	d
Decr 25th Ballance	4	12	3¼
1861 Jany 6th Small Hymn Book	~	1	6
20 Flat Do Do	~	2	6
From Children for Books	~	~	4
Feby 24th 2 Writing Books	~	~	6
Small Hymn Book	~	1	6
March 24th 1 Writing Book	~	~	3
July 14 - 3 Do - Do	~	~	9
[illegible] Collections	14	3	6
Aug 11th Small Hymn Book	~	1	6
Decr 8th 4 Writing Books		1	0
22nd for Childrens Books		7	0
	19	11	7¾
25th for Book	~	4	10
	£ 19	16	5
Expences of the year	13	2	9½
Ballance	6	13	7½

1861 Paid	£	s	d
Jany 2nd Coals	~	4	4
Feby 2nd Mr Stevenson for Hymn Books	1	0	5
12 Bibles at 2/6d each	1	10	0
Feby 8th Coals	~	3	6
1 Doz of Writing Books	~	2	0
9th Carriage of Bibles	~	~	6
13th Repairs done at Chapel	~	1	6
March 6th Post order	~	~	9
April 10th 6 gross of tickets	~	2	6
May 24th Burnswick Blacking	~	1	0
25th Pens	~	1	2
Candles Black Lead & Brush &c	~	5	3
June 22nd 1 Doz of Writing Books	~	2	0
July 6th Carriage of Hymns	~	~	4
28th Mrs Stephenson	~	5	0
Mr Holroyde	~	2	0
Aug 23rd Coals	~	2	8½
Hymns	~	13	6
26 Childrens Tea	1	1	8
Oct 12th Bow belonging the Bass new haired	~	1	6
14th 3 Ash pans repaired & carriage	~	5	2
Decr 19th Mr Johnsons Bill for Candles	~	8	10
Coals	~	4	0
21st Hymn Books	~	12	0
Mrs Marvin for Cleaning	1	10	0
Reward Books	3	11	0
Carriage of Hymn Books	~	~	2
2 Large Bibles for Children prize	~	10	0
25 Expences	£ 13	2	9½

Cross Hills account book in 1861 featuring the repair of the 'bass' (blocked in for clarity).

The subscribers raised the sum of £3-10-0d, but what exactly was this 'bass'? The dictionary describes it as being 'the fibre of the inner bark of the lime tree used for matting, etc. Was this the floor covering of the first chapel, used to cushion the coldness of the flagstones? Or were they prayer cushions or 'hassocks'? What-ever the use, they were obviously subjected to a lot of hard wear.

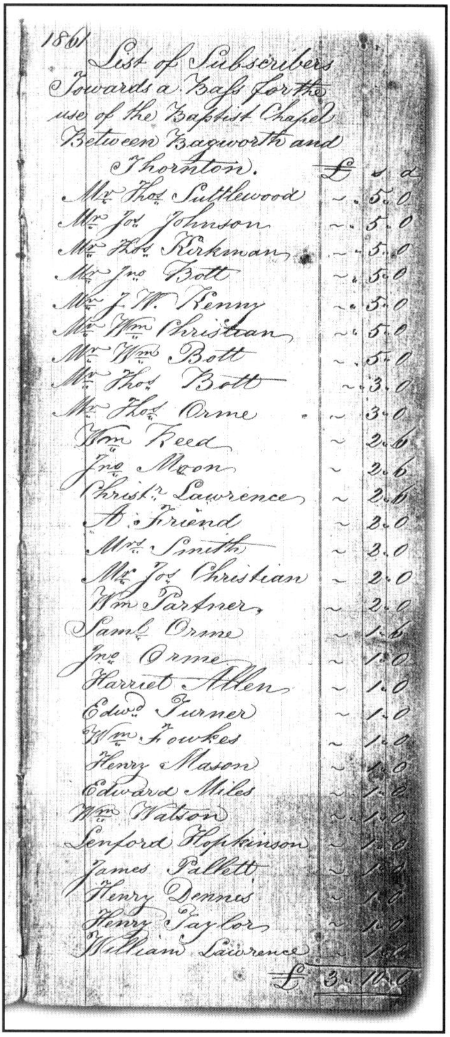
1861

List of Subscribers
Towards a Bass for the
use of the Baptist Chapel
Between Bagworth and
Thornton.

	£	s	d
Mr Thos Littlewood	–	5	0
Mr Jos Johnson	–	5	0
Mr Thos Kirkman	–	5	0
Mr Jno Bott	–	5	0
Mr J.W. Kenny	–	5	0
Mr Wm Christian	–	5	0
Mr Wm Bott	–	5	0
Mr Thos Bott	–	3	0
Mr Thos Orme	–	3	0
Wm Reed	–	2	6
Jno Moon	–	2	6
Christr Lawrence	–	2	6
A Friend	–	2	0
Mrs Smith	–	2	0
Mr Jos Christian	–	2	0
Wm Partner	–	2	0
Saml Orme	–	1	6
Jno Orme	–	1	0
Harriet Allen	–	1	0
Edwd Turner	–	1	0
Wm Fowkes	–	1	0
Henry Mason	–	1	0
Edward Miles	–	1	0
Wm Watson	–	1	0
Lenford Hopkinson	–	1	0
James Pallett	–	1	0
Henry Dennes	–	1	0
Henry Taylor	–	1	0
William Lawrence	–	1	0
	£3	10	0

Subscription list written in the back of the book in 1861 featuring the purchase of the 'bass'.

Each year the choir was paid '5/- for strings'. Were these 'strings' for the stringed instruments? They certainly owned a double bass, as it was kept under the choir stairs during the 1930's and '40's. And on May 14th 1920 there was an entry stating 'Repairing Double Bass— 15/-'.

Slates and slate pencils @ $1\frac{1}{2}$d each were used in the Sunday school to keep down the expense of purchasing fresh writing books, which in 1864 were 2/- per dozen.

Some brickwork alteration was also done in 1864, as 6s/6d was paid for materials, with 10/- for stepping stones.

There must have been washing facilities at Cross Hills in 1874, because $\frac{3}{4}$yd. of flannel was $5\frac{1}{2}$d and 1lb. of soap 5d! The only water available at this time was rainwater, presumably collected in a butt, as was usual.

Rev. Joseph Winks of Leicester, who died May 28th 1866, did the printing and sold books from a very early date, and he was strongly connected to the Baptist Movement. During 1875 Cross Hills paid him £7-1-0d for various books. Also in that year oil lamps must have started to replace candles, because several gallons of 'petroleum' was purchased at 2/-

per gallon. The petroleum would presumably be lamp oil of the kerosene type, not petrol as we know it. At 2/- per gallon it was quite expensive for the year of purchase.

The first audit of the Account Books was on January 26th 1882 when Mr. C. H. Kirkman signed the books as being correct. From 1863 regular annual payments of £2 and £3 were paid to Barton school, most likely for education costs. However, exactly what these payments were for is not recorded.

Lime was purchased presumably for lime washing (decorating) out the 1814 chapel. Original seating, probably benches, was replaced in 1857 at the time when the original Sunday school was 'rebuilt'.

DEEP HARMONY L.M. HANDEL PARKER, 1857-1929

SWEET is the work, my God, my King,
To praise Thy name, give thanks and sing,
To show Thy love by morning light,
And talk of all Thy truth at night.

2 Sweet is the day of sacred rest,
No mortal care shall seize my breast;
O may my heart in tune be found,
Like David's harp of solemn sound.

3 My heart shall triumph in the Lord,
And bless His works and bless His word:
Thy works of grace, how bright they shine!
How deep Thy counsels! how divine!

4 Then shall I share a glorious part,
When grace hath well refined my heart,
And fresh supplies of joy are shed
Like holy oil to cheer my head.

5 Sin, my worst enemy before,
Shall vex my eyes and ears no more;
My inward foes shall all be slain,
Nor Satan break my peace again.

6 Then shall I see and hear and know
All I desired or wished below;
And every power find sweet employ
In that eternal world of joy.

Isaac Watts, 1674-1748, *altd.*

A very popular Hymn sung in the early 1900's.

PART III

CHAPTER 6

THE FIRST 60 YEARS: 1885-1945

CROSS HILLS CHAPEL BUILDING NUMBER TWO

By 1883 the membership of the church, and particularly the Sunday school, had increased to such an extent that the oldest buildings had become inadequate. The decision was made to try and purchase an additional piece of ground at the back of the existing premises. Mr Joseph Johnson senior, from Bagworth, purchased 126 square yards of ground from farmer, Mr Geary, with the explicit intention of donating it to Cross Hills for a site on which to construct the new Sunday school .

In 1885 the old 1814 buildings were then demolished and a new church erected over the old site. An attached Sunday school was built on the newly donated ground to the rear.

The laying of the memorial stones was treated as a very 'grand affair', as can be gathered from the programme on page 46.

This event took place on Tuesday, July 21st 1885. The programme for the service, reads, 'Description of Contents of Bottle'. The time capsule, as the bottle is known, was discovered during demolition immediately beneath the first memorial stone on the lefthand side of the main entrance door. It was originally bricked in during construction about 113 years ago. The bottle was discovered by workmen during the dismantling of the 1885 church and it was purely by the hand of fate— or was it by higher authority?— that the glass container survived unbroken. For up to this point in time, no-one had the slightest knowledge of its whereabouts.

Contained in the time capsule, was a good descriptive letter of events in 1885 hand-written by Mr. George S. Johnson, aged twenty. He was the secretary of the Sunday school. It was George's father, Mr. Joseph Johnson, who purchased the extra ground and gave it for the benefit of the Sunday school.

The architect for the building was Mr. John Wills of Derby; Mr. William Needham of Loughborough was the builder. Total cost of the second church building was £1,100.

Shown is a letter of receipt from Joseph Geary, dated May 1st 1883, for the selling of land adjacent to Cross Hills church for a new Sunday school. It was bought by Joseph Johnson, Snr.

May 1st 1883

Received from Joseph Johnson Senior, of Bagworth in the County of Leicester, the sum of £5 (five pounds) as a deposit on or for 126 square yards of land at 2/6d per sq. yard bought of me, situated in the Parish of Thornton, and being at the end of the present General Baptist Chapel situated in the Parish of Thornton and known as the Cross Hills Chapel.

£5-0s-0d

May 1st 1883 Joseph Geary

(Sealed with an Inland Revenue stamp to the value of one penny)

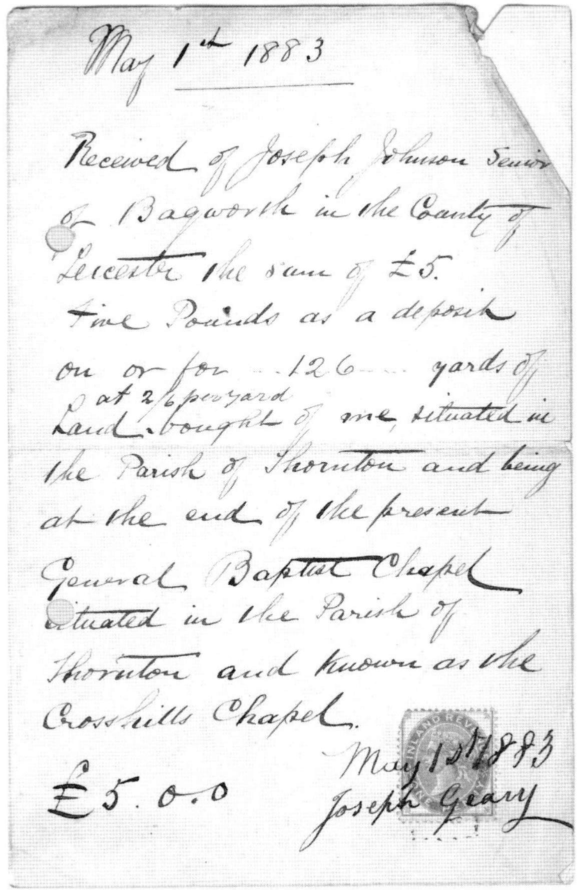
May 1st 1883

Received of Joseph Johnson Senior of Bagworth in the County of Leicester the sum of £5. Five Pounds as a deposit on or for 126 yards of Land at 2/6 per yard bought of me, situated in the Parish of Thornton and being at the end of the present General Baptist Chapel situated in the Parish of Thornton and known as the Crosshills Chapel.

£5.0.0

May 1st 1883
Joseph Geary

Receipt issed by farmer Mr Joseph Geary on May 1st 1883 to Mr Joseph Johnson, Snr. for land purchased for the new Sunday school.

An early photo of the 1885 chapel taken about 1907

Was this Lithograph produced by John Wills, Architect, before the church was built? Note the exact and fine detail of the building.

White House
Barlestone
May 1883

Dear Sir/ At the Church Meeting last Sunday it was agreed that the following names be Trustees for the new Peice of Ground at Bagworth Chapel viz

Saml. Deacon Barton Fabis Farmer
Thos. Deacon Barton Fabis Clock & Watch Maker
John Compton Newton Burgoland Farmer
James Cart. Osbastone Farmer

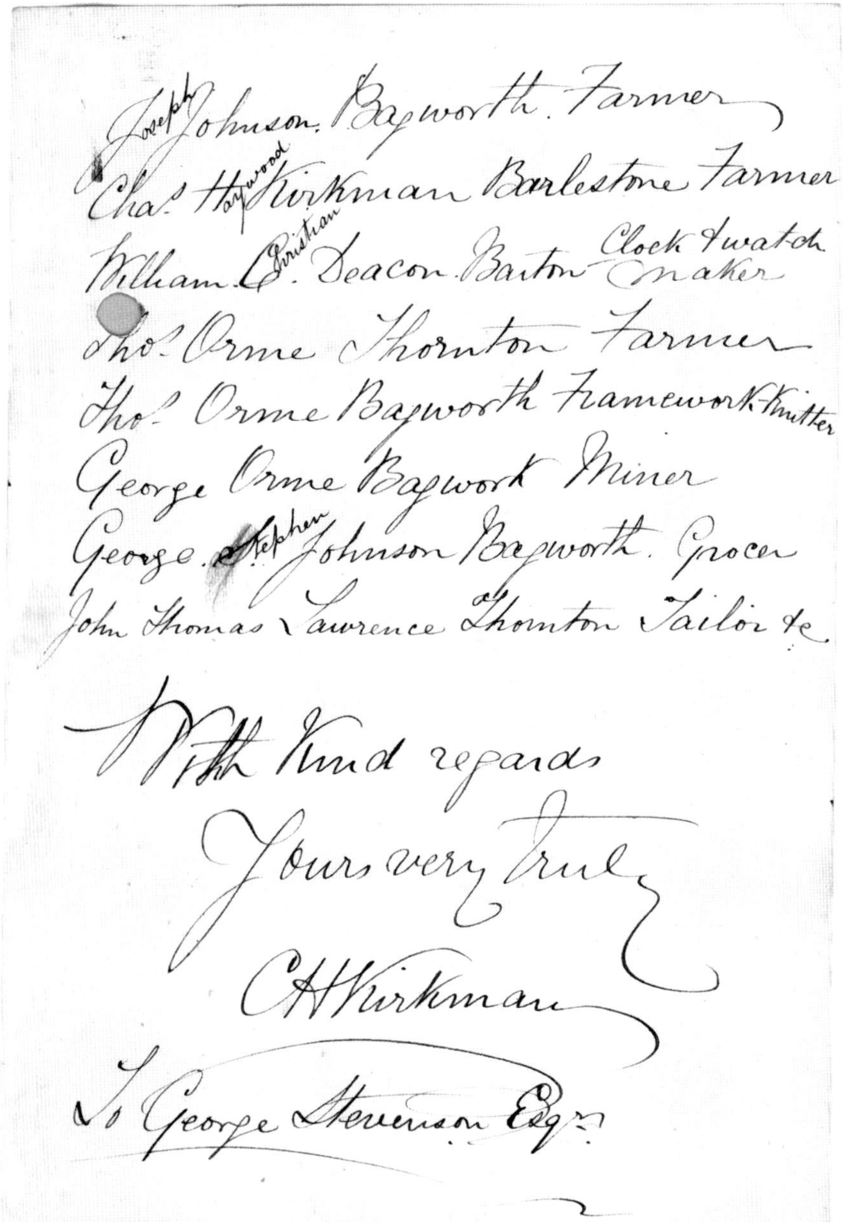

Joseph Johnson. Bagworth. Farmer
Chas. Haywood Kirkman Barlestone Farmer
William Christian. Deacon. Barton Clock & watch maker
Thos. Orme Thornton Farmer
Thos. Orme Bagworth Framework-knitter
George Orme Bagwork Miner
George. Stephen Johnson Bagworth. Grocer
John Thomas Lawrence Thornton Tailor &c.

With kind regards
Yours very truly
C H Kirkman

To George Stevenson Esqr.

Letter regarding the Trustees of the new piece of land:

Whitehouse
Barlestone
May 1883

Dear Sir,

At the Church meeting last Sunday it was agreed that the following names be Trustees for the new piece of ground at Bagworth Chapel:

Samuel Deacon, Barton Fabis, farmer.
Thomas Deacon, Barton Fabis, clock and watchmaker.
John Compton, Newtown Burgoland, farmer.
James Cart, Osbaston, farmer.
Joseph Johnson, Bagworth, farmer.
Charles Hayward Kirkman, Barlestone, farmer.
Thomas Orme, Thornton, farmer.
Thomas Orme, Bagworth, framework knitter.
George Orme, Bagworth, miner.
George Stephen Johnson, Bagworth, Grocer.
John Thomas Lawrence, Thornton, Tailor, etc.
William Christian Deacon, Barton Fabis, clock and watchmaker.

With kind regards
Yours very truly
C.H. Kirkman

To George Stephenson, Esq.

The programme lists the names of five of the men who laid the memorial stones:

1) Mr R. Kirkman
2) Mr Councillor G. Payne, Leicester
3) Mr Councillor Joseph Wilford, Leicester
4) Mr Edward H. Bott, Leicester
5) Joseph Johnson, Senr. Bagworth

Mr. John Orme of Bagworth also laid a memorial stone, making a total of six people participating in the stone-laying ceremony. It is not known why Mr Orme's name was excluded from the programme: perhaps it was an oversight.

LAYING

OF

MEMORIAL STONES

OF NEW

BAPTIST CHAPEL & SCHOOL-ROOM

BETWEEN

Bagworth & Thornton.

PROGRAMME

OF ARRANGEMENTS.

On TUESDAY, JULY 21st, 1885,

A PROCESSION

Will be formed at One o'clock near the Bagworth Colliery.

TIME OF SERVICE, TWO O'CLOCK.

BUCK, WINKS, AND SON, PRINTERS, LEICESTER.

Here to Thee a temple stand,
While the sea shall gird the land;
Here reveal Thy mercy sure,
While the sun and moon endure.

Hallelujah!—earth and sky
To the joyful sound reply;
Hallelujah!—hence ascend
Prayer and praise till time shall end.

DESCRIPTION OF CONTENTS OF BOTTLE.

THE

MEMORIAL STONES

WILL BE LAID BY

Mr. R. KIRKMAN, Cosby;

Mr. Councillor G. PAYNE, Leicester;

Mr. Councillor JOSEPH WILFORD, Leicester;

Mr. EDWARD H. BOTT, Leicester;

Mr. JOSEPH JOHNSON, Senr., Bagworth.

INTERVAL FOR COLLECTION.

HYMN III.

This stone to Thee, in faith we lay;
We build a temple, Lord, to Thee:
Thine eye be open, night and day,
To all who here shall bow the knee.

At Four o'clock

A PUBLIC TEA

Will be provided in a Tent.

TICKETS, ONE SHILLING EACH,

May be obtained of Mr. J. JOHNSON, Junr., Bagworth, and Mr. C. LAWRENCE, Thornton.

At Six there will be a

PUBLIC MEETING

In the Tent.

ADDRESSES will be delivered by Revs. W. EVANS, E. STEVENSON, C. HADDON, W. CHAPMAN, J. WATMOUGH, and F. PICKBOURNE.

There will be a Collection on behalf of the Building Fund.

Programme for the Laying of the Memorial Stones on July 21st 1885

CHAPTER 7

BURIAL GROUND

The Graveyard: Jacob Brewin, founder of Cross Hills; the Memorial Roll

The 'old graveyard' was probably purchased with the first (1814) chapel. The boundaries of this old burial ground are uncertain, but it probably extended from the front of the 1814 chapel to the road, and sideways to the small retaining wall which now separates the 'old graveyard' from the 'new graveyard'.

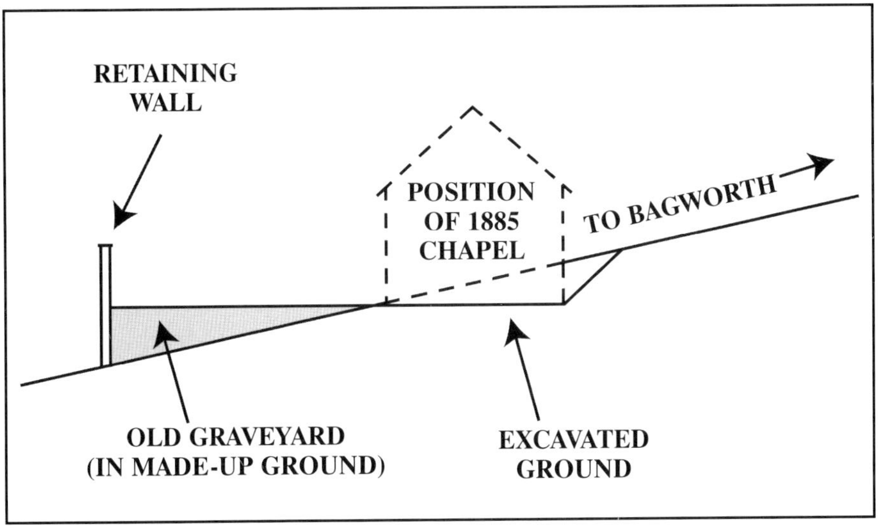

Sketch showing excavated and filled ground to prepare for the building of the church. Note the old graveyard is made-up ground.

Jacob Brewin: founder of Cross Hills

Jacob Brewin was instrumental in the building and formation of the Baptist church of Cross Hills. He was the chief founder and was interred in the first graveyard there. Indeed, his was the first recorded burial, as noted in the 'Memoirs of Samuel Deacon. (M.S.D.) — page 137.

Quote: 'Mr Jacob Brewin was buried at the chapel between Bagworth and Thornton on Feb 23, 1816, aged 60'. (See page 212 Memoir of Samuel Deacon)

Some early graves could have been built over when the 1885 chapel was constructed.

1) Jacob Brewin's Plaque (see above)

> **AS A TOKEN OF SINCERE RESPECT**
> **THIS MEMORIAL IS ERECTED BY A GRATEFUL PEOPLE**
> **TO PERPETUATE THE MEMORY OF**
> **JACOB BREWIN**
> **WHO, AFTER HAVING LABOURED FAITHFULLY**
> **SEVERAL YEARS IN THIS NEIGHBOURHOOD IN THE**
> **WORK OF THIS MINISTRY FELL ASLEEP IN THE**
> **ARMS OF HIS BELOVED LORD**
> **ON THE 23rd OF FEBRUARY, 1816,**
> **AGED 60**
> **Sublime his genius, and his manners sweet,**
> **His love was ardent, and his zeal was great.**
> **Peace spread her dove-like wings on his dear breast,**
> **'Twas there she reigned, and formed a settled rest.**
> **Sleep on, dear man of God, since now thy work is done,**
> **While we pursue the course thy pious feet have run.**

2) Thomas Cooper's plaque:

This plaque was **inside** the 1885 chapel, inferring that his grave was built over.

> **Beneath**
> **Are Deposited**
> **The Mortal Remains of**
> **Thomas Cooper Gent.**
> **Late of Hugglescote**
> **Who Departed This Life**
> **August 1st 1818**
> **Aged 92 Yrs**
> **Blessed Are The Dead Which**
> **Die In The Lord.**

3) John Boughton's Plaque reads:

> **Sacred**
> **To the Memory of**
> **John Boughton**
> **(Late Of Bagworth)**
> **Who Departed this Life**
> **Dec. 19th 1821**
> **Aged 59 Yrs.**
> **He Was, But Ah! What is He Now?**
> **The Future Judgment Must Declare;**
> **Consider Reader, What Art Thou?**
> **For Thou Must Meet the Saviour There;**
> **No Inquest on Thy Neighbour Take,**
> **But for Thyself Provision Make.**

THE GRAVEYARDS

There are two distinct sections to the graveyard: the **old** graveyard is pre 1906; the **new** graveyard is 1906 onwards. They are separated by the old original retaining wall.

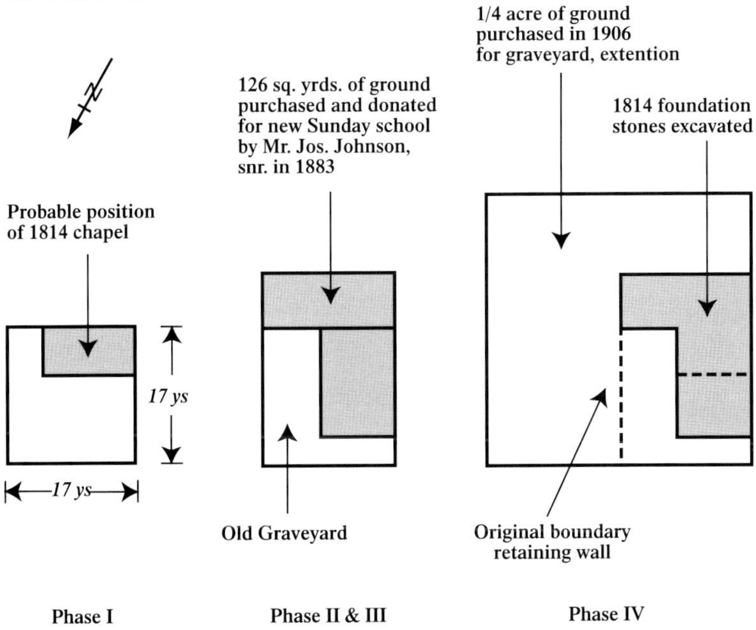

Plan showing the four phases of development of Cross Hills chapel.

Almost without exception, the only people known to be buried in the old graveyard are those who have memorial stones erected. Namely, Herbert Orme (4), Robert Radford, Eliza Radford, Nellie Moon, Thomas Orme (Superintendent of the Sunday school), Harriet Orme and Thomas Orme (the latter two buried in front of 1885 chapel near road), John Orme, Joseph Orme, Mary Henshaw, Annie Orme, Maria Elizabeth Marvin (aged 3).

The first person to be buried in the 'new graveyard' was Mrs Elizabeth Marvin, the mother of Tom Marvin. She died on April 9, 1907 aged 78. Her unmarked grave is situated at the bottom of the new steps on the left hand side, at the back of her son Tom's grave.

Many babies and children are buried in both graveyards, and a few people who were unfortunately killed in accidents at work.

Mary Elizabeth Richardson aged 3 years died on January 19th 1924, of a fever. Her sister Jessie Richardson aged 7 years died on September 23rd 1924, also of a fever. They lived in the cottage at The Park, Bagworth. Many years later their mother left the district to live elsewhere, and asked for the bodies of her children to be exhumed and reburied near to her new home. Permission was obtained from the authorities, but when digging commenced no remains could be found as so long a time had elapsed.

Cyril Hardy aged 15 yrs was killed in a lift accident in Leicester on February 7th 1926.Francis Richard Farmer aged 28 yrs was killed on March 29th 1910 whilst working at Bagworth station. John Rossell aged 19 yrs was killed underground at Desford pit on January 22nd 1927

In 1913 it became law to keep a register of all burials in graveyards and cemeteries, but at Cross Hills a register was not made until 1925 by the Rev. E. J. Garnham. On October 30th 1913 an entry was made in the Church minute book by The Pastor that '... to comply with the requirements of the Law, Burial Certificates should be kept by a duly authorised officer.' But no register was actually kept at Cross Hills until 12 years later.

Much research was done at Cross Hills to identify graves- most of the information coming from the epitaphs on the gravestones and from copies of death certificates that have been kept since 1913. Also from the many memorial cards which were popular at this time. From the results of the research, in 1953, a plan was drawn up by Mr. Peter Willett showing each individual grave with the name and date of burial. This plan is constantly updated to avoid future confusion.

Below are a few well known family names connected with the chapel, many more of whom are buried in Cross Hills graveyard. Orme, Lawrence, Rossell, Smith, Hextall, Prime, Willett, Gamble, Harris, Farmer and Jones are in the 20th century section of the graveyard.

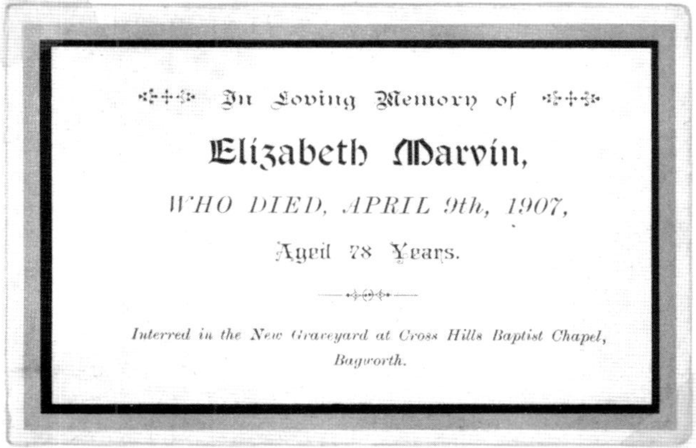

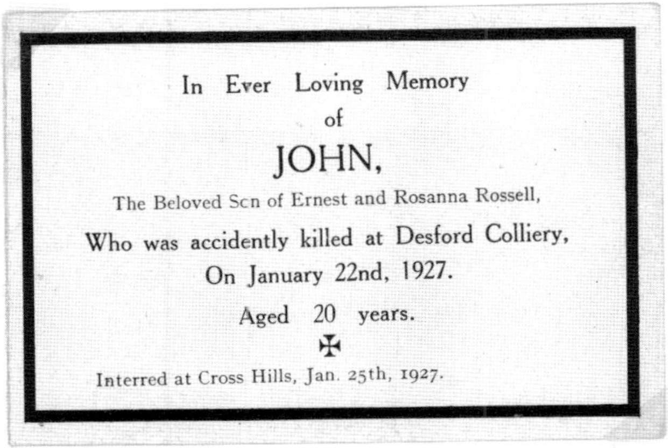

Example of Death Cards which were popular early in the century.

Pre 1900 no burial records exist, and only gravestones and plaques in the new church entrance refer to certain pioneers of the Baptist movement at Cross Hills. Some could have been buried under the 1885 chapel building.

Another Plot of Land for Burial

In May 1905 a long discussion took place regarding the potential acquisition of a plot of land adjoining the chapel, for use as a graveyard. Mr. Geary, the landowner, had been interviewed by members of the church, lead by the Senior Pastor. Unfortunately, the outcome of the meeting with Mr. Geary was unfavourable, as his asking price of 3/- per square yard was deemed by the committee as '... beyond all reason'.

It was felt that the landowner should be interviewed at a later date by Mr. C. Massey and Mr. Lawrence. This must have been a shrewd Public Relations operation, for when Mr. Geary was approached by the duo, the outcome was much more successful.

At a meeting on November 15th 1905 it was disclosed that Mr. Geary had arrived at a definite arrangement for the sale of a portion of his field, the price was now down to 2/- per square yard. Mr Geary was willing to sell a quarter of an acre of land to the church, so long as he could keep the mineral rights.

Photo of the chapel taken by Mr Tom Prime on the day of John Rossell's funeral, Jan. 25th 1927.

Mr. Geary was asked, on February 27th 1906, to get his solicitor to act with all haste in the transfer of the land. Also, he was told that the Church committee expected him to cut down the large tree growing in the hedge. A month later, members of the church meeting heard that Mr. Geary had still not cut down the tree. In view that the landowner had promised to remove the tree, Mr. Massey was urged to bring pressure to bear on him to do so in a reasonable time.

Mr. Massey reported on February 27th 1906 that Mr. James Hill was prepared to lend money to Cross Hills in order for them to complete the purchase of the new burial ground. The amount involved was

£157-5s-0d at $4^1/_2$% interest. It emerged on April 27th 1908, after checking accounts of the Burial Ground, that Mr. James Hill was still owed £161-9s-10d for his loan. The church would endeavour to bring the debt down to £100 by the end of May.

Landscaping the Grounds

Arrangements regarding the new wall were made as follows: it was agreed to take down the old wall in the centre and build a new wall on the outer side of the graveyard alongside of the road. The wall would be built in sections, to a height of 5 feet with a blue brick foundation and coping stones which would match existing ones.

Posts of oak were specified, and the style of the wrought iron double gates must harmonize with the five feet high wall.

The following Brethren *'were agreed to see along the fencing':* Messrs Hubbard, Massey, Lawrence, H. Orme and T. Orme, junior.

The junior pastor and Mr. Massey were asked to set out the specifications of work to be done at the new graveyard. The church would then invoke tenders from Mr. Thomas Insley for the ironwork, and Mr. Reuben Blower for the brickwork.

On October 4th 1906, it was decided that a set of steps would be added to the wall dividing the old graveyard from the new. A small fence was also due to be obtained to protect the side of the old graveyard, next to the path leading to the schoolroom. Along the centre of the new graveyard would run a four feet wide drive.

Opening of the New Graveyard

The opening of the new graveyard was set for the first Saturday in November, 1906. A great effort was made to secure the services of Arthur Orme of Bristol to perform the opening ceremony. It was felt that Arthur was the right choice, as he represented one of the oldest families working within Cross Hills Baptist Church. Unfortunately Arthur's services were unavailable at the time, so the duty fell on the second choice, his father, Senior Deacon of Cross Hills, Mr. Thomas Orme.

Mr Massey called a meeting on Thursday March 31st 1906 when the following Trustees were appointed:

Charles H Massey, Herbert Orme, Thomas Spencer, William Prime, Walter Bland, Thomas Walmsley, Thomas Orme, Harry Hubbard and John Farmer.

A bazaar held on February 10th 1909 raised £85-8s-9d, the proceeds of which went towards the *'extinction of debt existing on the Burial Ground account.'*

It was decided to press ahead with the 'ornamentation of the burial ground' at a meeting on March 12 1913. Twenty trees of various description would be planted, the planning of which was left to the discretion of the Burial Board.

Rev Darvell's Inauguration, Burial Certificates and the Law

Sunday October 26th 1913 was the day that Rev. F.C. Darvell was inaugurated into Cross Hills. He preached both in the afternoon and evening, with a view to the vacant Pastorate. The Pastor explained at the church meeting of October 30th that to comply with the requirements of the Law, the Burial Certificates should be kept locked in a secure place by a duly authorised officer connected with the burial ground. Until a safe could be obtained, the certificates would be in the custody of the Secretary.

The graveyard record book was founded by Rev. E.J. Garnham on March 25th 1925. The Burial Certificates and book were kept locked in a box in the Vestry. One key was kept at Mr. C. Massey's residence, Thornton, and the other at Mr. Jim Willett's, Bagworth.

Cross Hills Baptist Church Burial Fees

see item a) Total fee 18s-6d to be buried, in the 1920's.

Appointments and Resignations of Officers

Resignations of the Treasurer, J. Hill, and the Secretary, C. Massey, were impending at the meeting of September 12th 1907. New appointments for these posts were dealt with on January 24th 1908, when Mr. William Prime was appointed Treasurer and Mr. Abraham Willett became Secretary. Mr. Thomas Walmsley, the Sexton of Cross Hills, was voted to continue in his office during the current year of 1908, the conditions of service being that he be paid 6% of the total burial fee for each grave dug.

CROSS HILLS BAPTIST CHURCH,

between BAGWORTH & THORNTON.

BURIAL FEES.

		Total Fee.	Minister.	Digger.	Church
a.	For ordinary grave (Single 5 ft. 6 in. deep)	18/6	3/6	14/-	1/-
b.	For child under 12 years (Single 5ft. 6in. deep)	17/6	3/6	13/-	1/-
c.	For still-born child (Single 3 ft. 9 in. deep)	7/6	–	7/6	–
d.	Grave for 2 Interments (7ft. 6in.) 1st opening	19/6	3/6	15/-	1/-
	2nd opening	18/6			
e.	In case of persons not associated with the Church	30/-	5/-	14/-	11/-
f.	For selection of site, in each case if reserved in advance and paid for	3/-			
g.	Erection of head or footstone	3/-			
h.	For persons not associated with the Church	5/-			
i.	Extra for enclosure	10/-			
j.	For persons not associated with the Church	15/-			

NOTE.—Any INSCRIPTION DESIRED must be first submitted for the approval of the BURIAL BOARD.

Please apply for particulars to **Mr. J. FARMER,** 74, Station Road, Bagworth; Secretary of the Burial Board.

Treasurer to the Burial Board, Mr. WALMSLEY, Bagworth, to whom ALL FEES should be paid.

Sacred Songs and Solos:

Revised and Enlarged, with Standard Hymns.

TWELVE HUNDRED PIECES.

Compiled under the Direction of

Ira D. Sankey.

IN this Revised and Enlarged Collection of "Sacred Songs and Solos" will be found most of the old favourites sung by Mr. Sankey in the great Revival Meetings conducted by Mr. Moody during their three notable campaigns in this country; together with a number of new pieces which have more recently become popular, and many others now published for the first time.

"Sacred Songs and Solos" is the premier book for use at Conventions, Evangelistic and Fellowship Meetings, in Places of Worship, Sabbath-Schools, and Mission Halls. It is almost superfluous to say that "Sacred Songs and Solos" has found favour in all parts of the world where the English language is spoken.

'The Glory Song'

WHEN all my labours and trials are o'er,
And I am safe on that beautiful shore,
Just to be near the dear Lord I adore,
Will through the ages be glory for me.

Oh, that will be . . glory for me, . .
Glory for me, . . glory for me, . .
When by His grace I shall look on His face,
That will be glory, be glory for me!

2 When by the gift of His infinite grace
I am accorded in heaven a place,
Just to be there, and to look on His face,
Will through the ages be glory for me.

3 Friends will be there I have loved long ago;
Joy like a river around me will flow;
Yet, just a smile from my Saviour, I know,
Will through the ages be glory for me.

CHAPTER 8

OLD FAMILIES CONNECTED WITH CROSS HILLS

(A) THE BLOWER FAMILY OF BAGWORTH

Although there were very few houses in the two villages in the 1800's, large families made up for the population. We know that there were 125 pupils attending Cross Hills Sunday school in 1885.

One large family attending Cross Hills was the Blower's, who lived in a small cottage in The Square, Bagworth.

The Square, showing 'The Plough' public house and the cottage on the far right where David and Sarah Blower brought up twelve children.

BLOWER OF BAGWORTH

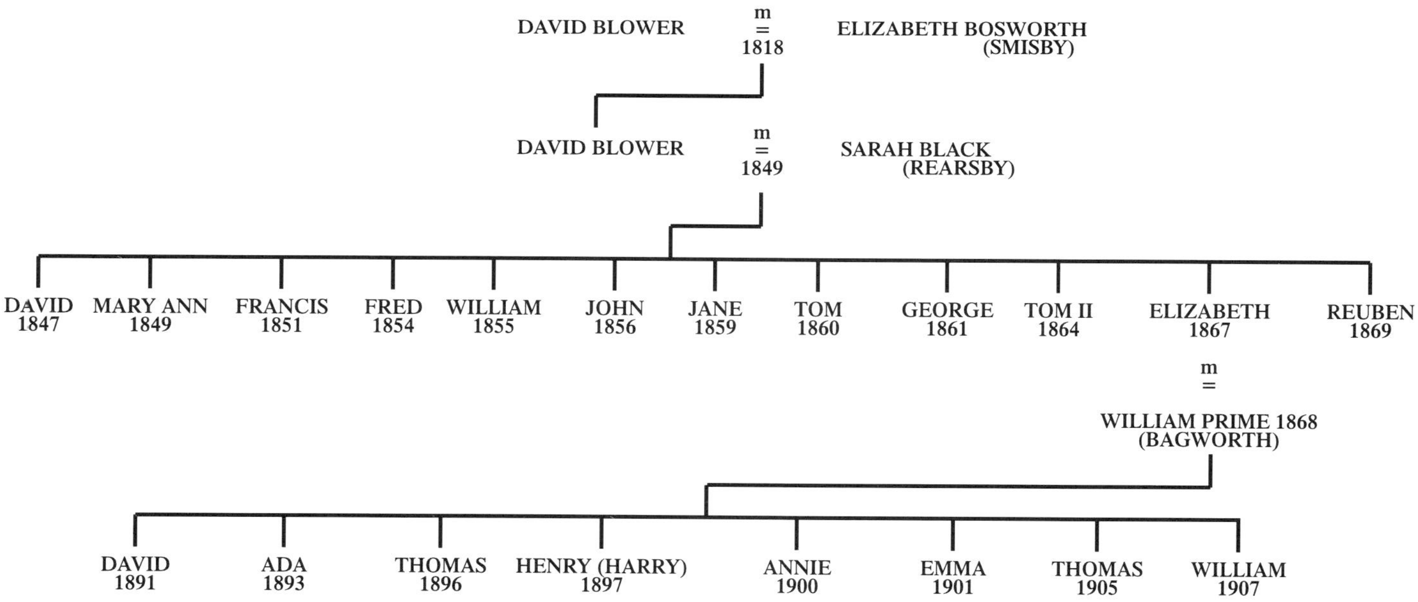

Blower Family Tree: from David and Elizabeth Blower

Mr David Blower, Snr. 1827 - 1881 who married Sarah Black in 1849. They had 12 children in 22 years.

Mrs Sarah Blower, 1824 - 1910, who brought up her 12 children in a tiny cottage in 'The Square', Bagworth.

Family Tree Branches Out

David, senior, was born at Bagworth and worked as an agricultural labourer. He married Sarah Black, from Rearsby, around 1849. They brought up their entire family in a small terraced cottage which also served as a shop in 'The Square' Bagworth, one living room down, two bedrooms up. These cottages still survive today.

David (1827 - 1881) and Sarah (1824 - 1910) became the parents of 12 children within 22 years, gaining one child approximately every other year. (see photo and family tree) But, unlike the 'old woman who lived in a shoe, who had so many children she didn't know what to do' Sarah sent them all to Cross Hills Sunday school for their 'further education'. The whole family became closely associated with the church over the years and, *'all grew up to be decent upright citizens'*.

Mr David Blower, Jnr. Local Preacher at Cross Hills Church.

John (Jack) Blower – local preacher, who 'put his beliefs before his animals'.

George Blower – engine driver who emigrated to the United States of America.

Mr Tom Blower with his racing 'Penny Farthing'.

David, junior, the eldest child, was born in 1847 and became a local preacher who preached regularly at Cross Hills.

Mary Ann kept a village shop and lived to be around 96 years old.

John came along in 1856 and also became a local preacher.

George was born in 1862 and became an engine driver whose duties included driving local trains through Bagworth on the Coalville to Leicester line. Railway men, like everyone else, were poorly paid, so the railway employees came together and decided to go on strike at a certain time, wherever they were, whatever they were doing. The critical time arrived for the strike just as George was driving his engine close to Cross Hills church towards Bagworth. He stopped his engine and, just to make sure nobody moved it, emptied the firebox down the embankment.

Unbeknown to George, the strike had been called off at the last minute and his employers fired him for his action. The long and short of it was, none of his 'workmates' backed him up, and not quite knowing what to do next, he emigrated to America and became an engine driver in Chicago. It was not until late in life that George saw fit to return to his homeland.

Thomas (born 1865) attended Cross Hills Sunday school and was presented with his prize of the Bible in 1876. Tragedy struck Tom's marriage early in life when his twenty-two year old wife, Ada, died in childbirth on December 22nd 1889. This was followed by the death of his baby on Christmas Day of the same year.

He became a 'champ' at racing penny farthing bicycles, winning many important races. After keeping the 'Cross Keys' public house in Loughborough for a time, he came back to Bagworth and became the landlord of 'The Plough Inn', where he unfortunately caught pneumonia and died in 1909. A large memorial stone cross stands in Holy Rood church yard at Bagworth in Thomas's honour.

Elizabeth Prime (nee Blower) – did not like being photographed! Note Tom's old penny farthing cycle as she pegs out the washing.

Elizabeth Blower (born 1867), the sister of Tom, married Cross Hills Choirmaster and Treasurer, William

Prime. Elizabeth was a Sunday school scholar at Cross Hills and became a teacher there (according to information inside the time capsule).

One thing she had never liked, was having her photo taken. But one day her sons photographed her pegging out the washing— leaning over the old penny farthing bicycle, as the photograph so ably illustrates!

William and Elizabeth went to Barton in the Beans in a horse and cart to be married. During the journey there was a snow storm which blanketed them, making it a truly 'white wedding'. Apparently the honeymoon was nothing to get excited about— just a day's outing in Leicester!

Elizabeth lived all her life in the same cottage in Bagworth 'on the hill'. She was born there in 1867 and died there on October 21st 1946, aged 79, having reared seven children all of whom attended Cross Hills.

They had four boys and three girls.

Reuben Blower was the youngest of the 12 (born in 1869). After passing through the Sunday school he became a carpenter and builder, and ran an undertaker's business in Ellistown. He was also a J.P. and Alderman. It was Alderman Reuben Blower who built the long brick wall in front of Cross Hills chapel graveyard.

When he died, his coffin was made by William Prime junior, his nephew, from solid oak cut from a tree which was grown in Bosworth Park.

Reuben, the youngest of the 12 Blower children, b.1869, rode to London on this Penny Farthing cycle. He was a carpenter, builder and undertaker at Ellistown and became a J.P. and Alderman.

REAL-LIFE STORY No 1

A tale of John Blower

John Blower, an old Cross Hills Sunday school scholar, and another brother to Tom and Reuben was, among other things, a 'local preacher'. He was also keen on showing his prize rabbits and poultry, and would travel quite long distances in his horse and trap in order to compete in these events.

As it happened, John Blower had a colleague living opposite him, who also liked to visit the shows and they would travel together.

John considered himself a very religious man who would never work on Sundays. One Saturday night, after travelling from a show, they arrived home very late. In fact it was after midnight, the early hours of Sunday morning, and rather than go against his beliefs and set about unloading the rabbits, poultry and unharnessing the horse, etc., he left everything in his yard just as it was. John went in home, making straight for his bed, much to the discomfort of all the animals, and the particular annoyance of his colleague who was left to do all the work himself

THE NEXT GENERATION
REAL LIFE STORY No. 2

To encourage the children to go to chapel, their mother (Elizabeth) used to send them off with a sweet each— called a 'nob of rock' in those days!

One Sunday afternoon they all queued up for their nob of rock, when their mother exclaimed, 'Oh, dear, I've run out of rock!' To which little Willie replied, 'Well, I'm not going to chapel then.'

'Oh, yes you are,' cried their mother. But defiant Willie ran off and lay down in the field called The Crewe at the top of the 'sand hole' to the rear of the cottage.

Now, his mother was not prone to give up that easily, and he knew that some form of punishment was in the offing. It was a hot afternoon and Willie lay facing the back door of his house so that he could see any approach by his furious mother. At last he got tired of lying on his right side and had to turn over. His mother, who had been watching carefully, crept up and seized him by the scruff of his neck. He was sent straight up to bed as punishment.

It so happened that day, the preacher at Cross Hills was Elizabeth's brother, David. Of course, as was the usual practice on such occasions, he came to tea. David enquired where little Willie was, and being told that he had been sent to bed without any tea for refusing to go to chapel, his uncle objected to the punishment. Elizabeth gave way and Emma, Willie's sister, was allowed to take his tea up to bed, at the same time seizing the opportunity to tease him by saying, 'How do you like being sent up to bed early, Willie?'

Not wishing to admit defeat, Willie replied, 'Oh, it's all right— actually I'm having a good rest!'

Unfortunately, his Mother heard the conversation and shouted up to Emma, 'If you don't come down at once, you'll be the next to be sent to bed!'

At that, Emma made a hasty retreat.

The late Sarah Blower's shop 1910.
Back (L-R): Ada Prime; Ada Gowdridge.
Front (L-R): Willie Prime; Hal Bland.

Mr Henry Prime (widely known as Harry) with his motorbike and sidecar.

Henry Prime

Henry Prime (better known as Harry) and Tom Prime (sons of Elizabeth Prime, nee Blower) became Deacons of Cross Hills, Tom holding the post of Treasurer for twenty-eight years. Both are credited with taking some of the photographs of Cross Hills chapel shown in this book. Annie, a sister, became assistant organist.

Harry took his bride-to-be, Susan, to be married at Barton-in-the-Beans in the sidecar of his motorcycle combination. He was a World War I veteran and spent a lot of his time working for the 'British Legion'.

A Cross Hills Ladies Sewing Class about 1905

(B) THE ORME FAMILY OF BAGWORTH AND THORNTON

As can be seen from the family tree, the Orme family goes back 'a long way' and as far as Cross Hills is concerned, 'all the way'.

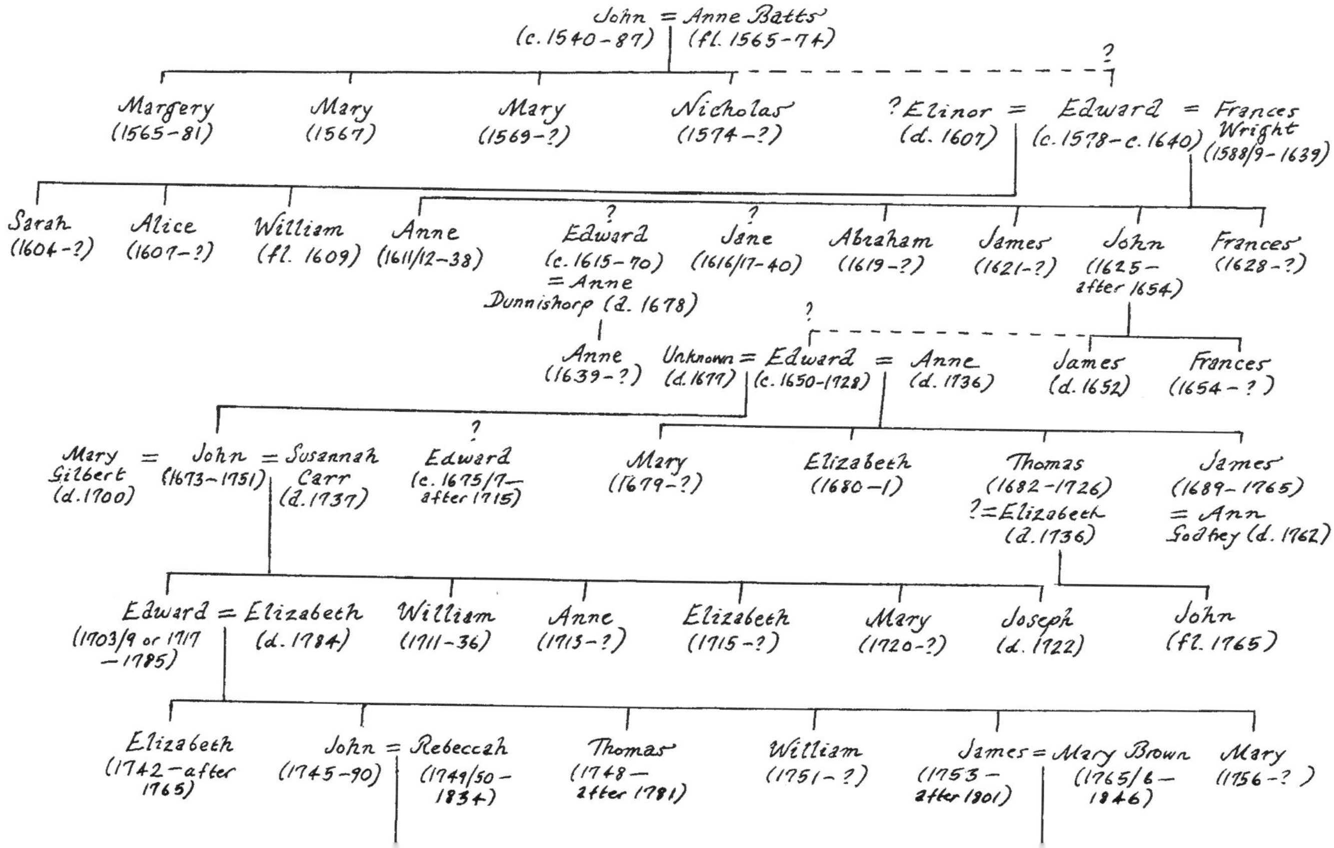

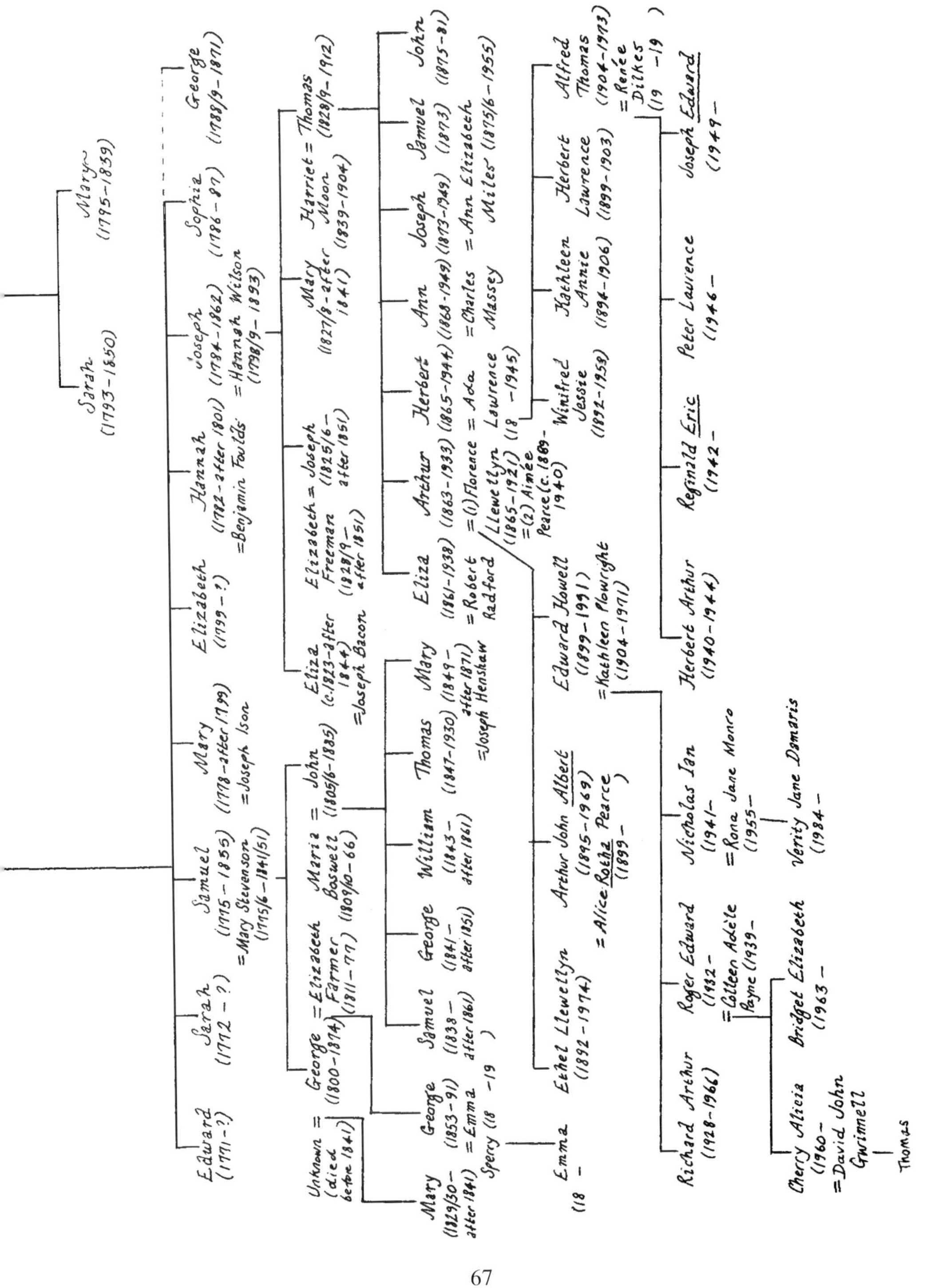

Sarah (1793-1850)
Mary (1795-1839)
Edward (1771-?)
Sarah (1772 - ?)
Samuel (1775-1855) =Mary Stevenson (1775/6-1841/51)
Mary (1778-after 1799) =Joseph Ison
Elizabeth (1799 - ?)
Hannah (1782-after 1801) =Benjamin Foulds
Joseph (1784-1862) =Hannah Wilson (1798/9-1893)
Sophia (1786-87)
George (1788/9-1871)
Unknown (died before 1841) = George (1800-1874) = Elizabeth Farmer (1811-77)
Maria Boswell (1809/10-66) = John (1805/6-1885)
Eliza (c.1823-after 1844) =Joseph Bacon
Elizabeth Freeman (1828/9-after 1851) = Joseph (1825/6-after 1851)
Mary (1827/8-after 1841)
Harriet Moon (1839-1904) = Thomas (1828/9-1912)
Mary (1829/30-after 1841)
George (1853-91) = Emma Sperry (18 -19)
Samuel (1838-after 1861)
George (1841-after 1851)
William (1843-after 1861)
Thomas (1847-1930)
Mary (1849-after 1871) =Joseph Henshaw
Eliza (1861-1938) =Robert Radford
Arthur (1863-1933) =(1) Florence Llewellyn (1865-1921) =(2) Aimée Pearce (c.1889-1940)
Herbert (1865-1944) = Ada Lawrence (18 -1945)
Ann (1868-1949) =Charles Massey
Joseph (1873-1949) = Ann Elizabeth Miles (1875/6-1955)
Samuel (1873)
John (1875-81)
Emma (18 -
Ethel Llewellyn (1892-1974)
Arthur John Albert (1895-1969) =Alice Rotha Pearce (1899-)
Edward Howell (1899-1991) =Kathleen Plowright (1904-1971)
Winifred Jessie (1892-1959)
Kathleen Annie (1894-1906)
Herbert Lawrence (1899-1903)
Alfred Thomas (1904-1973) =Renée Dilkes (19 -19)
Richard Arthur (1928-1966)
Roger Edward (1932- =Colleen Adèle Payne (1939-
Nicholas Ian (1941- =Rona Jane Monro (1955-
Herbert Arthur (1940-1944)
Reginald Eric (1942-
Peter Laurence (1946-
Joseph Edward (1949-
Cherry Alicia (1960- =David John Gwinnell
Thomas
Bridget Elizabeth (1963-
Verity Jane Damaris (1984-

The following has been edited from a letter to Peter Willett from Mr. Nicholas Ian Orme, who is Professor of History at Exeter University. He is the grandson of Mr. Arthur Orme and great grandson of Thomas Orme, senior.

1) Edward Orme, who died 1785, was parish clerk of Bagworth Anglican church. He was evidently a small peasant farmer who held or rented land locally. His son, John, who died 1790, was destined to an early death at forty-five years of age, leaving behind a large family. What occupation John followed I do not know, but it may have been a factor that his sons, in the early 19th century, were framework knitters or labourers.

Bagworth Manor was enclosed from 1474 and 2,000 acres of Parkland were fenced off. Enclosure is usually said to have caused peasant farmers to lose their livelihood because they had to pay legal fees and fencing costs, and their new allotments of only a field or two were not viable to support them like their old Common Rights on the open fields. I wonder, did the Baptist Revival in the village link in with these changes, in which the social status of people fell?

I think the Ormes must have become Baptists in the 1780's, because the children of John all had infant baptism in the church, up to Sophia in 1786. But I found no church record of infant baptism for his son, George (b.1788 or 1789) or for later members of the family, though they went on being married and buried in the church for some time. I have assumed that the change in my family's status and their becoming Baptists has nothing to do with the Industrial Revolution, because Viscount Maynard did not open a colliery in Bagworth till about 1826.

2) Thomas, Senior, (Whimsy Tom as he was known) was born at Bagworth 1828/29. He became a coal miner by 1851, colliery engine driver by 1860 and remained so until 1875, but in 1871 he had also opened a grocery shop in Bagworth. **By 1883 he had moved from Bagworth to Thornton** where he was described as a farmer from 1893 - 1904. The shop in Bagworth was eventually inherited by his daughter, Eliza, (who married Bob Radford), the shop being situated opposite Bagworth Church Lane.

Thomas was a prominent member of Cross Hills chapel from 1849, being successively, scholar, teacher, superintendent, deacon and steward. He became Chairman of Thornton School Board 1885 - '87 and Parish Councillor of Bagworth 1897 - 1900. He must have had a good deal about him to have progressed from fairly humble origins to local prosperity— I have always suspected that his uncle George, the **clockmaker,** who died unmarried in 1871, left him his estate and that this assisted Thomas's fortunes.

On his retirement he returned to live at Bagworth again, where he died on September 29th 1912.

3) Arthur, Tom's son, was born in 1863 and went to school in Bagworth until he was fourteen. The schoolmaster then said he had taught him all he knew!

The Ormes did not move to Thornton until the late 1870's/early 1880's.

Arthur must have been clever, because he secured a good job by the standards of the family in those days— as assistant clerk and steward of Leicester Borough Asylum, March 1877 until November 1884. In other words, he was a Junior Hospital Administrator. He then moved to be clerk and steward— **the leading administrator of Bristol City Asylum at Fishponds, Bristol, until 1925.** He married there, had three children and eventually remarried in 1923 after the death of his first wife in 1921. He spent his last years in Winscombe and Yatton, Somerset, and died in 1933. He was a man of great ability and charm and (as eldest son) exercised a good deal of influence in the family at Thornton, even while living at a distance. **Arthur remained a Baptist all his life, was a major figure at Foster Baptist Church, Downend, near Bristol, and is buried there.**

Arthur married a Methodist, and his children all became Anglicans though my Father, Edward Howell Orme, was quite happy in any kind of church or chapel, and was at various times churchwarden, organist and local preacher in quite a variety of them!

4) I certainly think that the Baptist Movement has played an important part in the social history of Bagworth/Thornton, as well as the religious history of the area, helping to mark (and minister to) the change from a largely agricultural society to a cottage industrial one.

Mr. Nicholas Orme

Although there seemed to be **two** families of Ormes at Cross Hills during the 20th century— one at Bagworth and one from Thornton— if we look back 'far enough' we see that both families descended from John (1745 - 1790) and his wife, Rebeccah (1750 - 1834), both of whom were living at Bagworth from long before the 1814 chapel was built. **It is more than likely, therefore, that Rebeccah was involved in the formation of the first Cross Hills chapel.**

They had nine children, and one of their sons, Samuel (1775 - 1855) had a son named John (1805 - 1885), who in turn was the father of 'Stockinger Tom'. This was the Bagworth, and main branch, of the Orme family. 'Stockinger Tom' was so nicknamed because he worked a weaving loom in his front room. As there were two Tom Ormes they were appropriately nicknamed to differentiate between them.

Another of the sons who was born to John and Rebeccah was Joseph (1784 - 1862). Joseph had four children, one of whom was named Thomas, (1828 - 1912) or 'Whimsy Tom' as he became known. This name stuck because he drove the winding engine (or whimsy) at Bagworth colliery. When he moved to Thornton, by 1883, the Thornton Ormes were established.

He and his wife, Harriett, did much good work at Cross Hills. They had seven children, all of whom attended the Baptist church at Bagworth— some, like Herbert, rising to Deacons or Officers.

A brass plaque in memory of Tom and Harriett was donated by their children and is now in the porch of the new church.

The plaque reads:

To the glory of God
and in loving memory of
Thomas Orme
who died Sept 29th 1912
aged 83 yrs
and
Harriett Orme
his wife
who died Dec 24th 1904
aged 66 yrs
Both devoted workers for this church and for
the extension of Christ's Kingdom.
This tablet is placed by their children by whom they
are still held in affectionate remembrance.
They rest from their labours.

1912

In Memoriam.

MR. THOMAS ORME, BAGWORTH.

THE Barton church has recently been called to mourn the loss of one of its best known and most highly esteemed members in the person of Mr. Thomas Orme, senr.; who passed peacefully away, after a brief illness, on Sunday morning the 29th of September. Mr. Orme was born at Bagworth in the year 1829, and was a member of a family honourably connected with the Baptist church in the village from its commencement. He was a scholar in its Sunday School, afterwards a teacher, and still later its superintendent. In early manhood he yielded his heart and consecrated his life to the Lord Jesus, and in 1853 with a number of others was baptized at Barton by Rev. W. Bott, who had then recently become co-pastor with the Rev. J. Cotton. In 1873 our friend was elected a deacon, and worthily sustained the office for the long period of nearly forty years. He was the last of the life deacons of the church, the system of triennial elections to the diaconate being brought into operation some years ago.

In the earlier years of his manhood our friend was an engine-driver at the Bagworth collieries, but he afterwards became a farmer at Thornton, where he continued to reside for thirty years. While there he became a member of the old School Board, and also served the public cause in other ways. Some years ago he retired and came to live in Bagworth again, and resided there until the time of his death. His funeral took place on October 2nd, when devout men carried him to his burial, amidst signs of respectful and loving sympathy shown by many who had known him. His mortal remains were interred by the side of those of his beloved wife in front of the chapel in which they had both long worshipped and loved so well. The present pastors—Revs. B. W. Owen and C. E. Palmer—with Rev. J. R. Godfrey, a former pastor, joined in the funeral service, the last mentioned giving a brief address in which the excellencies of the deceased's Christian character and conduct were dwelt upon. As a hearer and member of the church he loved the services of the sanctuary, rarely being absent either on Sunday or week evening. He was attentive and appreciative. He enjoyed and absorbed the great truths of the gospel as the preacher unfolded and applied them. And if he thought now and again that the method of presenting truth might be improved his suggestions were made in such a genial kindly manner as to be welcomed rather than resented by the preacher. As a worker in the Sunday School in earlier years he was diligent and devoted, aiming to make it a true nursery to the church. As a deacon he was wise in counsel, genial in manner, peace-loving in disposition. He would often have views of his own as to the best church policy to adopt at a given time or to achieve a desired purpose, but never imagined himself to possess all the wisdom in the world so as to override the views of others. There was no masterfulness of spirit in him, but a readiness to yield to the properly presented and calmly considered views of his brethren. Unlike Diotrephes he cared nothing about having the pre-eminence. He was also given to hospitality. For long years the pastors were welcomed to his home whether he lived at Thornton and Bagworth, and pleasant was the Christian intercourse had at such times. He was a pastor's friend, his whole attitude being helpful to the work of the ministry, the progress of the cause of God, and the upbuilding of the Church. One could have absolute confidence in him, in his uprightness of character, in his devotion to the welfare of the Church, in his loyalty as a friend. His pastor could say of him as Paul said of his Philippian friends, "I thank my God upon every remembrance of" him. His membership of the church extended through the long period of sixty-three years, and practically the whole of it was spent in close connection with it—as teacher or superintendent of the Sunday School, or deacon; and through the whole of it also he secured the love and esteem of his brethren, not only in Bagworth and Thornton, but in the whole area of the Barton church.

The nature of his brief final illness, which was attended by a lack of consciousness, prevented him from bearing testimony to his abiding confidence in Christ as his Saviour, yet his whole spirit and life had said up till then, "I know whom I have believed, and am persuaded that He is able to keep that which I have committed to Him against that day"; and so we rejoice that though he is absent from the body he is present with the Lord.

On Sunday, October 6th, Rev. B. W. Owen preached a memorial sermon at Bagworth to a good congregation, basing his remarks on Phil. i 21, "For me to live is Christ, and to die is gain."

J. R. G.

The obituary shown was written by J.R. Godfrey (Pastor) on the death of Tom Orme, Senior.

Some of the seven children of 'Whimsy Tom' and Harriett:

Eliza (1861 - 1938) married Robert Radford (Deacon of Cross Hills). Eliza owned a sweet shop in Bagworth village, near School Lane. Their large gravestone is shown here:

Arthur (1863 - 1933) moved to Bristol and married Florence Llewellyn. A Communion table was donated by him, in 1933. This is still in use in the new 1996 church.

The inscribed brass plaque on the table says,

> 'Presented to
> The Cross Hills Baptist Chapel
> by
> Mr. Arthur Orme
> in Memory of his Parents
> 1933

One of the memorial stones in the 'Old Graveyard'.

Arthur Orme moved to Bristol and donated a Communion Table to Cross Hills.

Herbert (1865 - 1944) who was deacon at Cross Hills, married Ada Lawrence. He was a farmer and kept a village shop in Thornton, which still exists today.

Ann (1868 - 1949) married farmer Charles Massey (Deacon and Secretary) and lived at Reservoir Farm, Thornton.

Six of the seven children of 'Whimsy Tom' and Harriett Orme are interred in Cross Hills burial ground.

Mr. Herbert Orme's shop, on the left.

And the old Methodist Chapel on the right – converted into Reading Rooms.

Back row, left to right: Winnie Orme, Annie Orme (nee Miles), Joe Orme
Front row: Ann Massey (nee Orme), Charlie Massey, Aimée Orme (nee Pearce), Arthur Orme and Ada Orme (nee Lawrence).

John Orme (1805 - 1885)

In the book of Deacon's Memoirs, *'Preacher, Pastor, Mechanic'* written in 1888, it states that during the building of the 1885 chapel *'Mr John Orme, who was a scholar in the Sunday school when the **first** chapel was reared, seventy years later laid one of the Memorial Stones of the **second** chapel, feeling almost like good old Simeon, who long had waited for the consolation of Israel, and 'ere the roof was on, passed away to his eternal rest.'* There is also an entry in Samuel Deacon's successors' personal subscription list book, (researched in the Records Office, Wigston, Leics.) stating that in 1827 John Orme gave 4/- (four shillings) towards alleviating the debt on Barton and Bagworth meeting houses.

Also in one of Deacon's receipt books of 1809, there are records of an 'Orme of Bagworth' who was sold a 30 hour clock for £5-15s-6d.

'Stockinger' Tom Orme (1847 - 1930) (Sunday School Superintendent)

As was his normal practise, Tom Orme (Stockinger Tom) walked from Bagworth to Cross Hills church many Sunday mornings, along with a group of children who were members of the Sunday school. Tom loved to be with children and loved the countryside. Indeed, he was an expert in his own right on wild flowers and the animals. As the happy party walked towards the church, Tom would educate the children in matters of Nature.

One day, he was pointing out plants and wild flowers when they saw a herd of grazing cattle. 'Observe how the cattle graze,' he said. 'See how they brush the many buttercups aside while they are eating. These animals never eat a buttercup by choice— because they sense that these plants are poisonous to their system.' Thus, Tom Orme would confer a worthwhile lesson in Nature to the children before they arrived at Sunday school, where they learned about Jesus.

Mr. Thomas Orme, junior, 'Stockinger Tom' complained on February 10th, 1910, that the sum of 15/- per annum he was paying for grass cuttings from the burial grounds was too expensive. After giving consideration to the matter, it was decided to let him have same for 5/- per year.

Another Sunday school incident for which 'Stockinger Tom' Orme was renowned.

One Sunday school anniversary day, it was raining the proverbial 'cats and dogs' and the children were feeling a bit depressed with the foul weather. They were not in the mood for singing at all on their special day.

Tom Orme, who could understand the children's feelings, stood at the end of the gallery and said, 'Children, I know it's raining hard outside, but listen to those birds singing, don't they sound beautiful?'

If anyone could influence the children and uplift their spirits, Tom could do it. He said: 'If those little birds can sing so sweetly out there in the rain, I'm sure you children can do so, too.'

Sure enough, the children immediately 'took heart' and sung of their very best.

Tom Orme was also renowned for concocting 'homemade medicines'. For cuts and bruises he made an ointment which people called 'Tom Orme sauve, or salve'. For coughs he made lozenges, which tasted so vile that people would spit them out when he was not looking.

He was also a bee keeper, and he always owned one cow, which he grazed in a nearby field. When it came round to milking time, he brought it home where it was housed in a shed in his back yard, which was situated at the bottom of 'School Hill' at Bagworth.

Cross Hills in the 1920's. Photograph taken with Harry Prime's Kodak plate camera.

C) THE MASSEY FAMILY OF STANTON-UNDER-BARDON & THORNTON

MASSEY OF STANTON UNDER BARDON & THORNTON

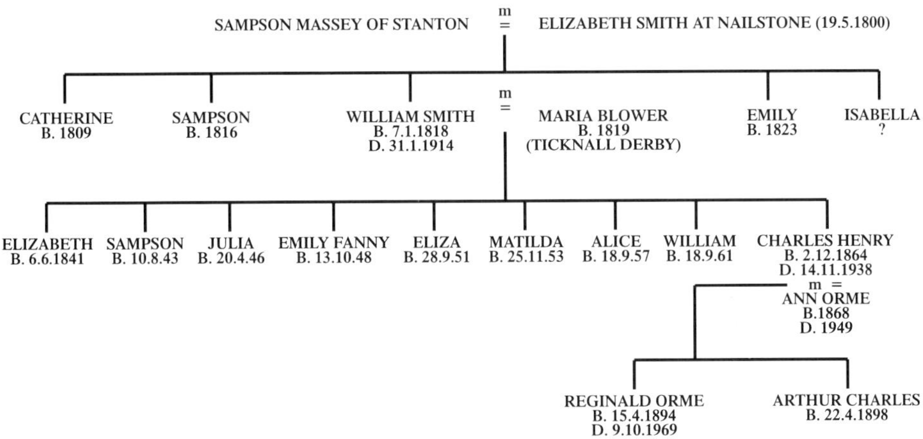

This simple family tree has been built up from a very old 'Family Bible' which was printed in 1796. It belonged to Mr. Sampson Massey of Stanton-under-Bardon, who presented it to his son, William Smith Massey, in 1840.

He married Maria Blower of Ticknall, in Derbyshire, and they had nine children. The last child, Charles Henry Massey (b. 1864 - 1938) married Ann Orme (1868 - 1949). They had two children, Reginald Orme Massey (1894 - 1969) and Arthur Charles Massey (b. 1898)

Charles was a deacon and secretary at Cross Hills. His wife was a prominent member of the Baptist church and both children attended the Sunday school.

A photograph of the family Bible showing the recordings of the births of his children can be seen here.

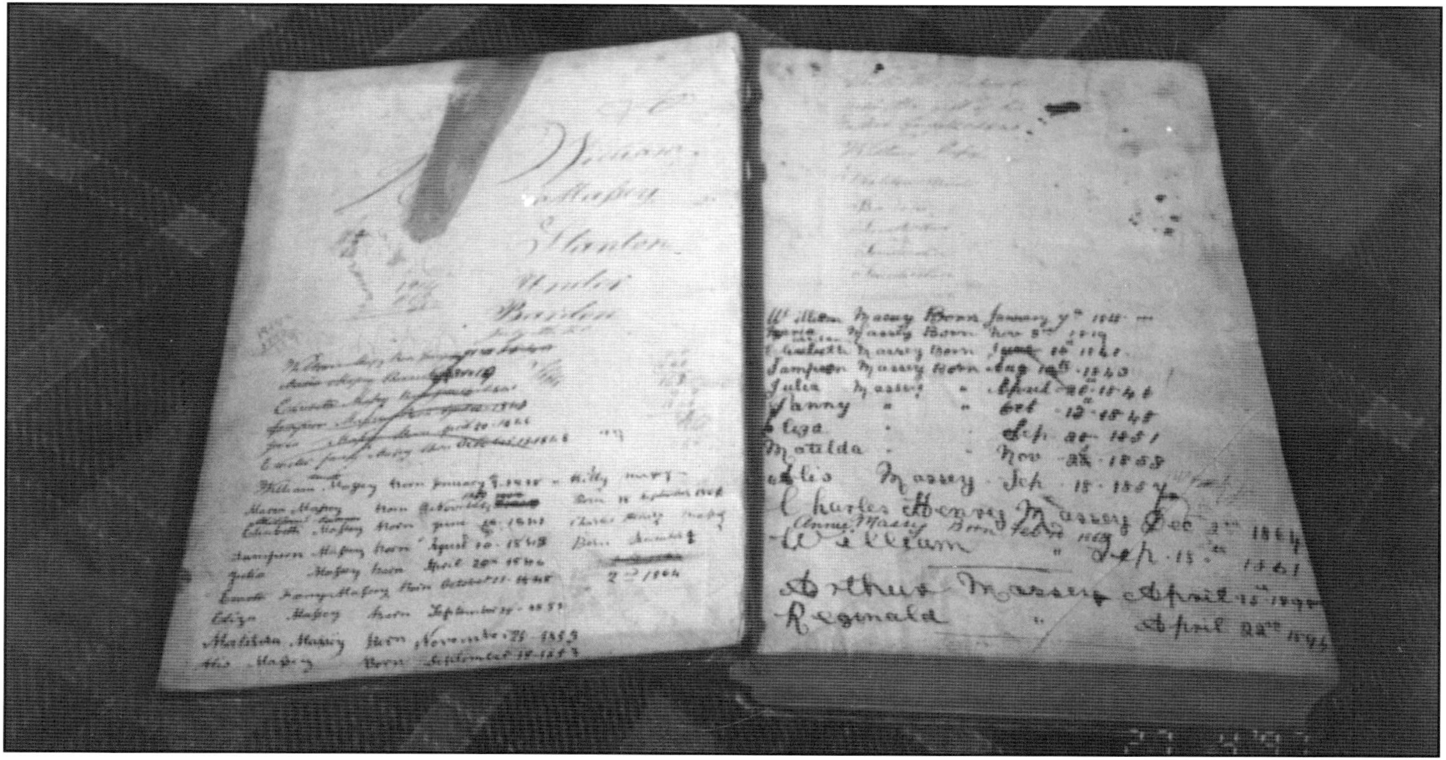

The Massey Family Bible – presented to Mr William Smith Massey,
of Stanton-under-Bardon, in 1840 by his father Mr Sampson Massey.

Below is a postcard sent by Charlie Massey before sailing to America. It was sent to his brother-in-law, Herbert Orme, requesting the hymn 'Eternal Father strong to save' to be sung for him at Cross Hills .

It looks, from his writing, as though he had a touch of the 'butterflies in his stomach'. Perhaps he did not like the look of the boat, or had he the fate of the 'Titanic' in mind?

One imagines that Charlie Massey's chosen hymn was sung at chapel as requested, because he returned home safely!

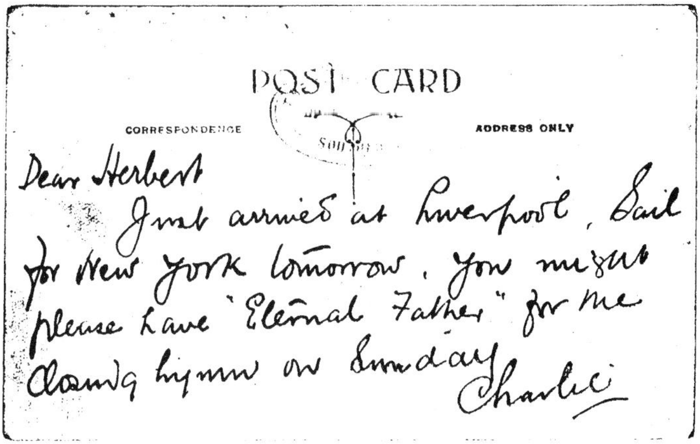
POST CARD

CORRESPONDENCE ADDRESS ONLY

Dear Herbert
Just arrived at Liverpool. Sail for New York tomorrow. You might please have "Eternal Father" for me closing hymn on Sunday
Charlie

THE C.S.S.M.
(CHILDREN'S SPECIAL SERVICE MISSION)

CHORUSES

This was a well used song book. The children sang favourite choruses such as:-

232

Jesus died for all the children, all the children of the world;
Red and yellow, black and white, all are precious in His
sight,
Jesus died for all the children of the world.

236

Joy, joy, joy, with joy my heart is ringing;
Joy, joy, joy, His love to me is known;
My sins are all forgiven, I'm on my way to Heaven,
My heart is bubbling over with His joy, joy, joy.

243

Two little eyes to look to God,
Two little ears to hear His Word,
Two little feet to walk in His ways,
Two little lips to sing His praise,
Two little hands to do His will,
And one little heart to love Him still.

252

God has blotted them out, I'm happy and glad and free;
God has blotted them out—I'll turn to Isaiah and see;
Chapter forty-four, twenty-two and three;
He's blotted them out, and now I can shout—
For that means me!

704

The wise man built his house upon the rock,
The wise man built his house upon the rock,
The wise man built his house upon the rock,
And the rain came tumbling down;
And the rain came down and the floods came up,
The rain came down and the floods came up,
The rain came down and the floods came up,
And the house on the rock stood firm.

The foolish man built his house upon the sand,
The foolish man built his house upon the sand,
The foolish man built his house upon the sand,
And the rain came tumbling down;
And the rain came down and the floods came up,
The rain came down and the floods came up,
The rain came down and the floods came up,
And the house on the sand fell flat.

CHAPTER 9

THE FIRST CROSS HILLS MINUTE BOOK

J R Godfrey's First Minute Entries

The first reference, in the earliest minute book, is written by Rev. J.R. Godfrey, who signs the first entry as senior Pastor of the Barton group of churches. The following introduction by him shows his concern of the importance of keeping records of meetings for the benefit of successive generations at Cross Hills Baptist Church:

Bagworth Baptist Church is a branch of the Church at Barton Fabis, but it is thought by the friends advisable to have a book in which minutes of proceedings of this section of the church can be entered separately, for guidance of the friends from time to time, and for the information of the generations following. The following, being the first minutes, are of a meeting held last Autumn.

signed J. R.. Godfrey Senior Pastor.

Rev. J.R. Godfrey presided at the meeting held in the schoolroom on November 20th 1899. We find that a resolution was passed, in line with other churches in the group, contributing the Harvest Festival proceeds of £5-6s-5d to the Mother Church at Barton Fabis.

Hearty and sincere thanks were given to all the friends who helped to clear off the debt on the chapel and school, which had recently been accomplished. It was decided to ask Mr. T. Marvin and the choir to kindly arrange for another concert in the coming year.

The following names, among others, were deemed worthy of a place on the Memorial Roll of the 20th Century Fund: Jacob Brewin, Christopher Lawrence, Thomas Cooper, Samuel Orme and Joseph Johnson. This was attributed to their long and beneficial connection with the cause of God, here at Cross Hills church. Jacob Brewin and Thomas Cooper are commemorated on slate plaques in the porch and in the lobby of the new 1996 Cross Hills Church.

Church Maintenance Committee

The following people formed the Committee at this time: the Pastors, the Deacons, and Messrs. Tom Orme, George Sperry, C. Massey, James Hill, H. Hubbard, C. Lawrence, H. Orme, T. Marvin, R. Radford, Wm. Reed and Thomas Walmsley. Please note that the latter's surname was Johnson; i.e. Thomas Walmsley Johnson, but to distinguish him from several other Johnsons, people simply knew him as Walmsley.

In April of 1905 it was agreed that some sort of appreciation was due to Mr. Thomas Insley for giving up much of his time overseeing the renovation of the chapel. To mark the good work Mr. Insley was to be privately presented at Shackerstone, by the Pastors, with a suitably engraved umbrella. The duties of collecting subscriptions for the umbrella were undertaken by Mr. Herbert Orme and Mr. Lawrence.

Mr. Massey Resigns From the Diaconate

The Church was about to see several changes occur in 1921, and by the meeting of October 13th, Mr. C. Massey had resigned from the Diaconate. Tributes were paid to him by Committee and members alike, who expressed the hope that 'ere long he might be again in active service'. Running parallel with this, it was recognised the need had arisen for the services of a third Minister in the Group of Churches. The Rev. E.J. Garnham explained that an additional Minister must be procured to serve here at Bagworth.

Mr. Walmsley gave notice of his intention to resign the post of Caretaker and Gravedigger.

The Communion Cups

Prior to the 1950's the key to the safe where all the deeds and important documents were kept in Barton chapel, was lost. When the safe was finally opened most of the paperwork had decayed and had disintegrated through age and dampness. However, solid silver communion cups were retrieved and each of the chapels in the group received one.

The Cross Hills cup is of an 'Irish Pattern', and is marked, London 1777, and weighs 9 ounces. But it is not used at Cross Hills, however, as passing around one cup for everyone to drink out of is not very hygienic. For this reason Cross Hills has always used individual glass cups since February 1st 1915, when 64 individual cups and two trays were purchased for £2-7-0d.

The Cross Hills 'Irish Pattern' Communion Cup.

PART IV: MUSIC AND SUNDAY SCHOOL

CHAPTER 10

MUSIC

Bandsmen: Tom Marvin

As already stated, music played a very important part of the Cross Hills chapel, and Tom Marvin was the organiser and conductor when the choir was in its 'heyday'.

Some of the more important musical occasions and events in the calendar of Cross Hills are: Easter; Sunday school anniversary; Harvest Festival and Christmas carol singing. For example, 'Messiah', 'Creation', 'Judas Maccabaeus', 'Samson' and 'Elijah', and many more oratorios were performed with orchestra.

For oratorios, professional soloists took the leading roles. These professional stars were engaged by Cross Hills specially to perform in our little church. Special staging was erected in the chapel— it reached from the Baptistry, over the pulpit and up to the Sunday school room to accommodate the large choir and orchestra. The choir master, Tom Marvin, was largely responsible for organising this. The Hymn book used for ordinary services was the Baptist Church Hymnal, but several 'Tune' books were used for the accompaniment, which contained many fine tunes. e.g. Ancient and Modern, Methodist Hymn Book, Alexanders, Bristol and the Sankey were used by the organist, who would pick the 'best' or most popular tune to fit the hymn.

Mr. Tom Marvin, Deacon & Choirmaster: the 'Grand Old Man of Music'.

Below is a programme of Handel's Oratorio, 'Judas Maccabaeus', performed on March 14th 1908 with a band and chorus of 60 performers.

Bagworth Baptist Chapel.

A Grand Concert

Will be given in the above Chapel,

On SATURDAY, MARCH 14th, 1908,

When Selections from

HANDEL'S ORATORIO,

"Judas Maccabæus,"

Will be rendered by

A Band and Chorus of 60 Performers.

PRINCIPAL VOCALISTS—

Miss Ellen Wilby, L.R.A.M., Soprano

Miss Lettie Nourish, Contralto

Mr. Haywood Dennis, Tenor

Mr. Dan Choyce, Bass.

Concert to commence at 6.30 p.m.

CAXTON PRINTING WORKS, IBSTOCK

Instrumentalists.

First Violins—
MR. FEARNS, A.V.M.I.C, and MR. HOLMES.

Second Violins—
MR. MASON and MR. CLARKE.

Viola—MR. BAYLISS.

Violoncello and Bass—
MR. HEMSLEY and MR. A. BURTON, (2nd V.B. Staff. Reg.)

Flute—MR. A. CLARKE, A. Mus., M.I.C.

Oboe—MR. BURTON.

Clarionet—MR. THORNLEY.

Horn—MR. F. MARVIN.

Cornet—MR. E. MARVIN.

Euphonium—MR. W. SPENCER.

Leader of Band—MR. FEARNS, A.V.M.I.C.

Organist—MR. NEWMAN.

Conductor—MR. THOS. MARVIN.

Tom Marvin, who was a miner at Bagworth colliery, was the founder of Bagworth Brass Band. He was loved by everyone, as he was quite a character. Tom liked a pint of beer, and sometimes when a string of notices were announced during a service he would slip out, down to the **'Stag and Castle'** the public house in 'the hollow', for a quick one, then return for the Sermon— no doubt with a ruddier complexion!

It might be of interest to mention at this stage something of the site of the Stag and Castle. This was before the bridge was built, which later took the railway overhead. At this time there was a simple level crossing at the pub, which was, in its time, a 'request stop' platform for passengers on the Leicester and Swannington Railway.

The manager of Bagworth colliery, Mr. Emmerson, (Tom's boss) once told him that he should not have any drink whilst at the chapel teaching children. Tom replied, 'My lad, it's not what goes in your mouth that defiles you— it's what comes out!'

Tom Marvin's grandchildren believe that he was a 'self taught' musician, and a good organist and composer— especially when he had a drink. He used to say that the 'twigs on the trees' reminded him of music.

CHOIRMASTERS

Tom Marvin retires

When Thomas Marvin retired as Choirmaster, December 6th 1916, Mr. W. Bland the Assistant Choirmaster took over. In valued recognition, Mr. Marvin was made Honorary Choirmaster. A subscription list was opened with a view to presenting a testimonial to the esteemed choirmaster for his long and faithful service to the church.

By February 20th, 1917, the sum realised was £4-17-10d, with which it was proposed to buy Mr. Marvin a chair inscribed as follows: *'Presented to Mr. Thomas Marvin by the Members and Friends of the Cross Hills Baptist Church for long service as Choirmaster. March 3rd 1917.'*

He was also presented with an inscribed ebony baton. He later gave back the baton to the chapel, which was used by successive conductors on special occasions. The baton, which is no longer used, has been presented to Tom's great grand-daughter, Mrs Julie Watson.

His grandchildren have kindly donated a new brass plaque, which has been mounted in the entrance porch of the new church in memory of him. Tom Marvin died on May 13th 1931 aged 74 years.

Mr. Walter Bland was Tom Marvin's successor, but the choir did not like his approach and abrasive manner and he was asked to resign.

Mr Walter Bland: the Choir did not like his approach.

Mr. William Prime:

Another Bandsman, Mr. William Prime of 'The Square' Bagworth, became a successful choirmaster of Cross Hills for 20 years, besides holding the post of Treasurer. Bandsmen and conductors wrote out and transposed music by hand, which they still do to a lesser degree, an arduous and laborious task back in those far gone days.

See samples of hand written music by Mr W. Prime. The music was composed by Mr. Henry Dennis, a farmer from Hugglescote, near Coalville, who attended Hugglescote Baptist Church situated in what is now Dennis Street. (Named after him)

Mr. William Prime, Deacon, Choirmaster, & Treasurer, of 'The Square' Bagworth.

ANNIVERSARIES

The Messiah: Handel With Care

Sunday school anniversary services were the most important occasion of the year. The music, which played a large part, was practised weeks before the event. The children at Cross Hills were split into two groups; the girls would learn the soprano or main part, whilst the boys would learn the alto part, separately at first (usually on a different midweek evening). Not until the parts had been thoroughly learned would they be brought together in harmony.

The choir also had an important part to play, as they sung anthems as well as helping the children occasionally. One unique feature of the Cross Hills anniversary was the finishing of the services with Handel's 'Hallelujah Chorus' from 'The Messiah'. Of course, everyone in the chapel stood up as is the custom. With a full choir of about 40 or 50 people, the organ and orchestra playing at full capacity, it was an impressive performance and high in decibels. Three bars from the end there was a sudden stop, 'rests' in the music, and it caught the children out talking when there should have been complete silence.

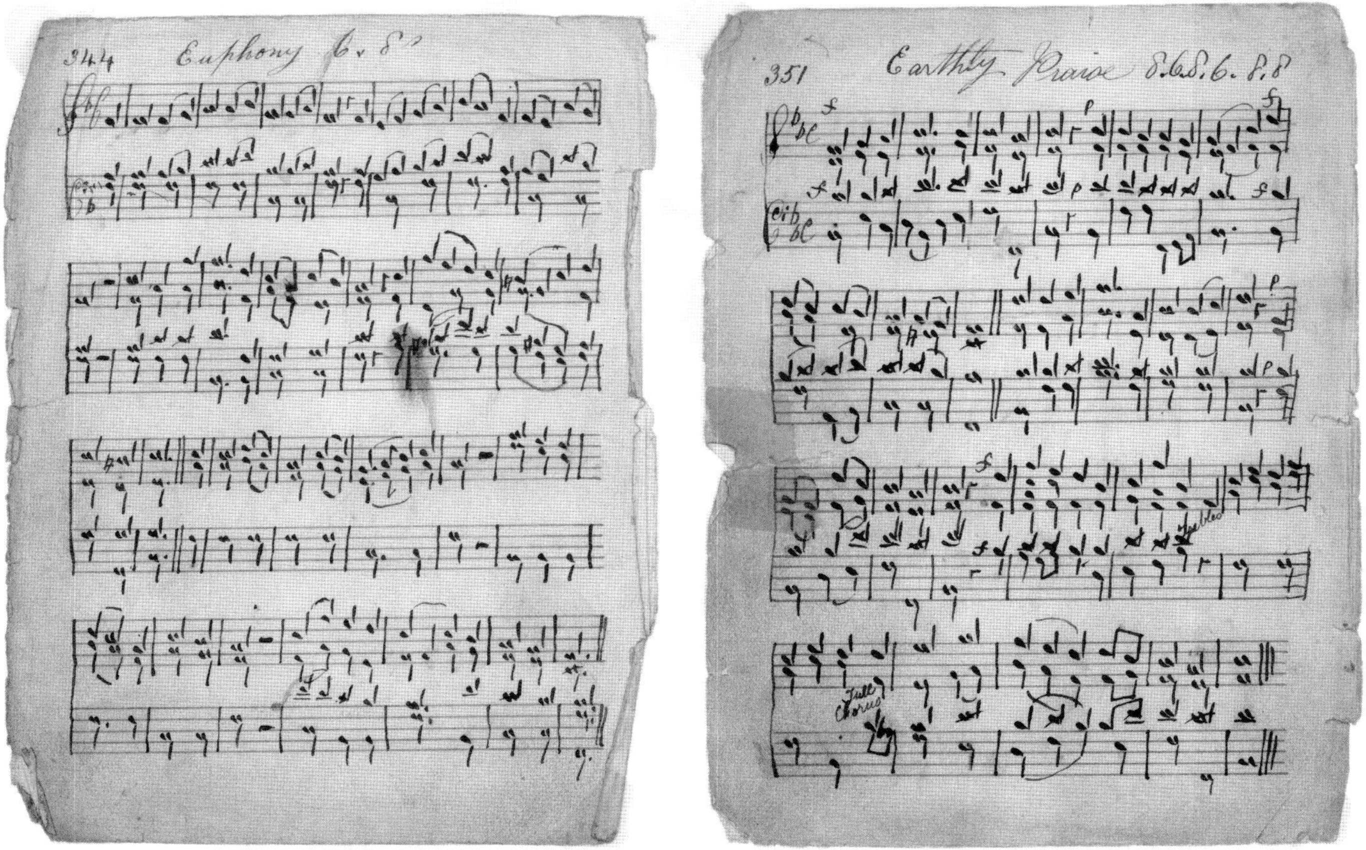

A sample of hand-written music transcribed for orchestra by Mr. W. Prime for two of Mr. Henry Dennis's compositions.

Helpers came from miles around, and would be entertained and fed at teatime by members of the chapel in their own homes, or in the Sunday school room if their house was not big enough.

The orchestra usually consisted of the organ, 1st and 2nd violin, cello, double bass, clarinet and trumpet or cornet. Being classed merely as amateurs, they met only on the Sunday morning's rehearsal before the performance. Needless to say, quite often 'peculiar sounds' could be heard as they struggled to harmonise.

It was a day of great 'feasting' as all the family descended for the occasion. Mothers had been busy baking, making trifles, jellies and other treats. Of course, everyone had to be dressed in their Sunday Best. The children, especially, made a very pretty spectacle sitting together, or 'sitting up' as it was called, and performing to their best ability.

A special speaker was usually invited to preach at both the afternoon (2.15pm) and evening (6.00pm) services. The freewill offerings taken at the services on this special day took the children on their summer outing (treat). The 'Buffs' (Royal Antediluvian Order of Buffalos) were also invited. They sat on the baptistry facing the congregation, proudly displaying their medals and regalia.

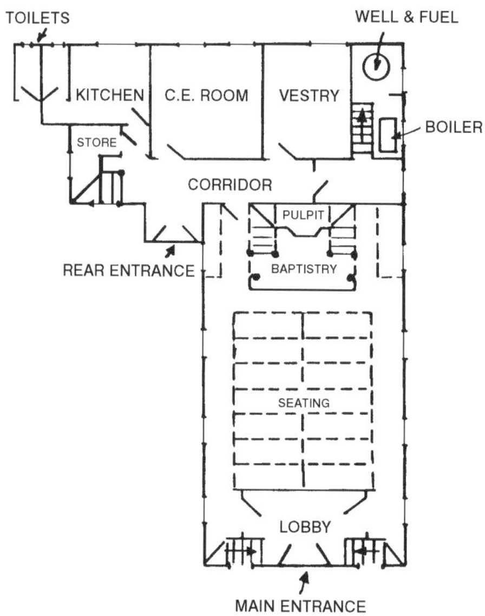

– **Ground Floor Plan** –

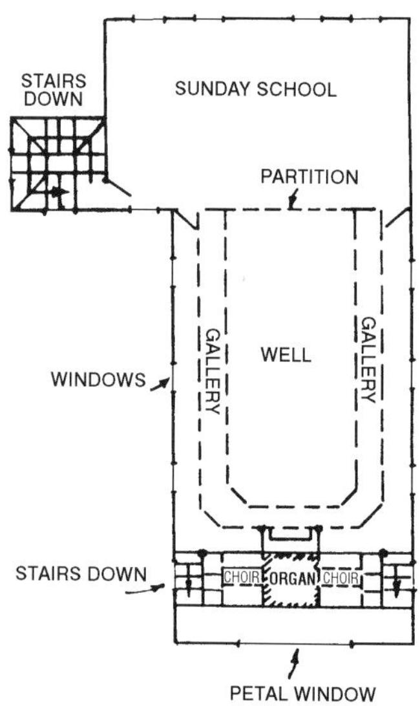

– **1st Floor Plan** –

Sketch plan of the 1885 chapel showing first floor and ground floor.

COMPOSERS

Henry Dennis (1818 - 1887) was a prolific composer of chapel music. Hymn tunes like 'Euphony' (1850), which were originally sung to 'Sweet is the work' and 'Earthly Praise' (1858), and also sung to 'Tis sweet o God, to sing Thy praise' were sung regularly at Cross Hills. Henry Dennis excelled at composing beautiful music for children, which was sung mainly at Sunday school Anniversary Services— or Sermons, as they were known.

Mr. Henry Dennis 1818 - 1887; Hugglescote farmer, fine composer and musician.

When the children 'sat up' for the Cross Hills sermons, girls sat on the Bagworth side and boys on the Thornton side. Children were 'graded' in size along the galleries, with the tallest at the back. The band accompanied them to inspiring hymns such as 'The Beautiful Harbour of Heaven' which rang out from Cross Hills at anniversary time, and which was always held on the last Sunday in May.

Plaque to the memory of Henry Dennis in Hugglescote Baptist Chapel:

To the Memory of
HENRY DENNIS : 1818 - 1887
A GIFTED MUSICIAN AND COMPOSER
THE PIONEER OF SCHOOL ANNIVERSARY MUSIC
30 YEARS SECRETARY OF THIS CHURCH
A SUPERINTENDENT OF THE SUNDAY SCHOOL
AND A FOUNDER OF THE DAY SCHOOL 1852
'LET US NOW PRAISE FAMOUS MEN......
SUCH AS SOUGHT OUT MUSICAL TUNES......
THEIR NAME LIVETH TO ALL GENERATIONS.'

Rev. R D Browne

Rev. Browne, 1905 - 1996, was an assistant minister as a young man in the 1920's. He composed a hymn which was included in the Baptist Hymnal, number 576:

'Thou Lord, hast given Thyself for our healing;
Poured out Thy life that our souls might be freed.
Love, from the heart of the Father, revealing
Light for our darkness and grace for our need... '
etc.

R. D. Browne.

J. L. W. (Les) Hill

Les Hill, as he was well known, of Newbold Verdon, composed several hymn tunes. One, which can be sung to the hymn shown, is called 'Cross Hills' and can also be sung to the hymn 'It is a thing most wonderful'.

One of Mr. Les Hill's compositions: This Hymn is called 'Cross Hills'.

Lynda Joy Kelly

Lynda Kelly, is a composer and an organist at Cross Hills. She is the wife of Cross Hills Pastor Garry Kelly and they live at Barwell, near Hinckley, Leics.

Lynda has won a competition for one of her hymns. Another of her very moving hymns, 'The Hem of His Garment', is sung at Cross Hills chapel. Her latest composition is printed at the back of this book.

The Hem of His Garment

Lynda Pryce

Lynda Joy Kelly's moving Hymn, 'The Hem of His Garment'.

2. Won't you touch the hem of His garment,
Won't you feel the power within,
Won't you kneel at the feet of the Saviour?
He can cleanse your soul from sin.
He'll set your feet on a rock,
Lift you out of the miry clay,
If you'll just touch the hem of His garment;
Reach out today.

Chorus

Reach out, reach out to Jesus,
The man from Galilee,
This man who makes the lame to walk
Has done so much for me.

3. Reach out in faith to Jesus,
Don't let Him pass you by.
The blessings His love can give you
Will last eternally.
Reach out in faith to Jesus,
Then trust Him through and through.
This man who makes the lame to walk
Can do so much for you.

Chorus

Reach out, reach out to Jesus,
The man from Galilee,
This man who makes the lame to walk
Has done so much for me.

CHAPTER 11

EARLY 20th CENTURY FUND RAISING

A sale of work took place on November 16th and 17th 1910, when nett receipts totalled £33-16s-0d to support the Leicester Royal Infirmary. Cross Hills gave regular donations to the hospital by putting on functions such as these.

The services on Harvest Festival Sunday, September 29th 1912, were taken by Rev. C.E. Palmer and Mr. David Blower.

When it was learnt that new fireplaces would be required for both vestries, the acquisition of the units fell to Mr. Massey who could obtain them at cost price. The installation task was assigned to Oliver Dilks.

The following gives an insight into the real fear of attack from World War I enemy planes. It was proposed by H. Orme and seconded by Mr. Butler, on October10th 1916, that all church property be insured against damage by aircraft.

Thanks were tendered on 20th March 1920 on behalf of the Church, to Mr. and Mrs. Butler for the gift of table linen to be used at Communion Services.

Enter Rev Garnham

On Wednesday June 21st 1920 Rev. E.J. Garnham presided at his first Cross Hills Church Meeting.

The Rev. E. J. Garnham was the much loved minister of the Barton Group of churches for 34 years (1920 - 1954). He was a very dedicated and sincere man who worked hard for the Barton churches. The Barton Group included Barton, Barlestone, Bagworth (Cross Hills), Newbold Verdon, Bosworth and Congerstone.

For a long period of time there was no assistant minister, and he travelled the circuit on his bicycle, whatever the weather. His work for the Cross Hills chapel will always be remembered and appreciated.

The Rev. E.J. Garnham, much loved Minister of the Barton Group.

On Saturday, December 5th 1953, a tea was held in the Sunday school room at Cross Hills in his honour, and an evening service was held at 6.30pm. Members and friends had been invited to contribute envelopes containing monetary gifts towards Mr. Garnham's retirement. These were hung onto a 'gift tree' and were opened during the evening service.

The memorial to the late John Farmer manifested in the form of a Pulpit Bible, dedicated August 28th 1955 on Anniversary Day by Rev. E.J. Garnham.

Treats

The Church's Cycle Club was granted permission to announce from the pulpit, notice of a meeting to organise the annual summer outing.

A School Treat was planned for July 7th 1928. It was, quote, *'left in the hands of Mr. J. Farmer to see Mr. Shepherd about booking the field.'* Mr. Shepherd owned nearby Park Farm, which still stands close to the bottom of Stephenson's railway incline on the Leicester and Swannington Railway.

In the 1920's games in the field opposite the chapel were often organised, and a special tea laid on.

During World War II, when petrol was scarce, Abbey Park was the favourite choice for an outing. But after the war, outings became more adventurous, and as many as six or seven bus loads would weave their way snake-like to places such as Skegness, Mablethorpe or Hunstanton from Cross Hills.

CHAPTER 12

SUNDAY SCHOOL

Robert Raikes, of Gloucester, was credited with founding the Sunday school movement in 1780. His portrait hung on the wall at Cross Hills for many years. He envisaged a great need for children to be educated, not only in the basics that were taught in day school— which were very primitive at the time— but from a Christian point of view.

Most children loved Sunday school, as the approach was quite different from the general learning procedure in day schools. The atmosphere was always relaxed and friendly. There was no cane, no rapping of knuckles with the ruler, no lines to write or other punishment that went with early general education techniques.

The activities were mainly Bible readings, looking at religious pictures and a lot of singing— hymns and choruses from special books. In the early days, pictures were displayed on a scroll called a 'picture roll' and cost £1 each. These portrayed biblical scenes and would be held up for the children to see, whilst the teacher told the story.

Large framed pictures also adorned the walls. Two of them in Cross Hills Sunday school illustrated 'Jesus the Good Shepherd' and 'Daniel in the Lions Den'. The whole Sunday school was highly organised, and a strict check on attendance was kept, not only of children but also the teachers.

In 1880 medallions were struck to Commemorate the Centenary of Sunday schools. On one side of the medallion was the portrait of Robert Raikes, and the obverse side showed mothers bringing children to Jesus. (Mark X v.14)

Sunday school started at 10.15am and finished about 11.30am. If scholars attended the afternoon service at 2.15pm their 'star card' was marked accordingly. The value of the 'prize' which was awarded at the end of the year depended on the scholars age and how many attendances they had made. Examples are recorded of Sunday school meetings where the actual value of 'one star' was fixed. e.g.— 1/2d per star, or 3 farthings per star for a 12 year old scholar.

As scholars grew older they were sometimes taken also to the night service too, making attendances of three times in one day. There was little time in those days for youngsters to get into mischief, but Sunday school did not seem to do any harm. In fact, most scholars grew up into good, honest and reliable citizens. Some joined the Church, and one or two spent their lives, after leaving the Sunday school, as missionaries overseas, spreading the gospel that they had first learned of at Cross Hills.

Here are examples of some attendances taken from the Cross Hills Sunday school registers:

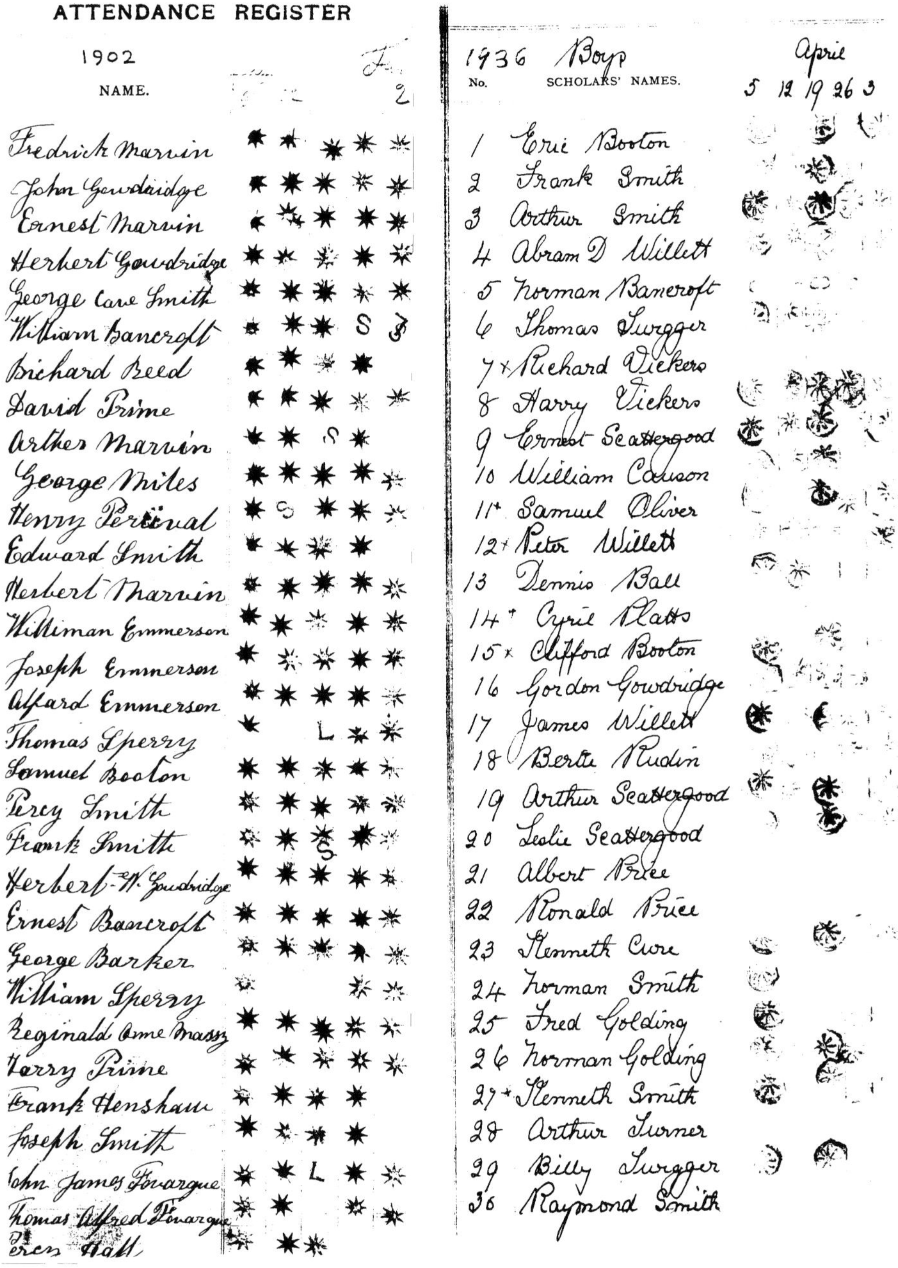

ATTENDANCE REGISTER

1902

NAME.

Fredrick Marvin
John Gowdridge
Ernest Marvin
Herbert Gowdridge
George Cave Smith
William Bancroft
Richard Reed
David Prime
Arther Marvin
George Miles
Henry Percival
Edward Smith
Herbert Marvin
Williman Emmerson
Joseph Emmerson
Alfard Emmerson
Thomas Sperry
Samuel Booton
Percy Smith
Frank Smith
Herbert W. Gowdridge
Ernest Bancroft
George Barker
William Sperry
Reginald Anne Massy
Harry Prime
Frank Henshaw
Joseph Smith
John James Fovargue
Thomas Alfred Fovargue
Percy Hall

1936 Boys — April 5 12 19 26 3

No. SCHOLARS' NAMES.

1 Eric Booton
2 Frank Smith
3 Arthur Smith
4 Abram D Willett
5 Norman Bancroft
6 Thomas Swgger
7× Richard Vickers
8 Harry Vickers
9 Ernest Scattergood
10 William Cawson
11× Samuel Oliver
12× Peter Willett
13 Dennis Ball
14× Cyril Platts
15× Clifford Booton
16 Gordon Gowdridge
17 James Willett
18 Bertie Rudin
19 Arthur Scattergood
20 Leslie Scattergood
21 Albert Price
22 Ronald Price
23 Kenneth Cave
24 Norman Smith
25 Fred Golding
26 Norman Golding
27× Kenneth Smith
28 Arthur Turner
29 Billy Swgger
30 Raymond Smith

Sample of Boys Attendance Register Books – for years 1902 & 1936 in which Sunday school pupils win stars.

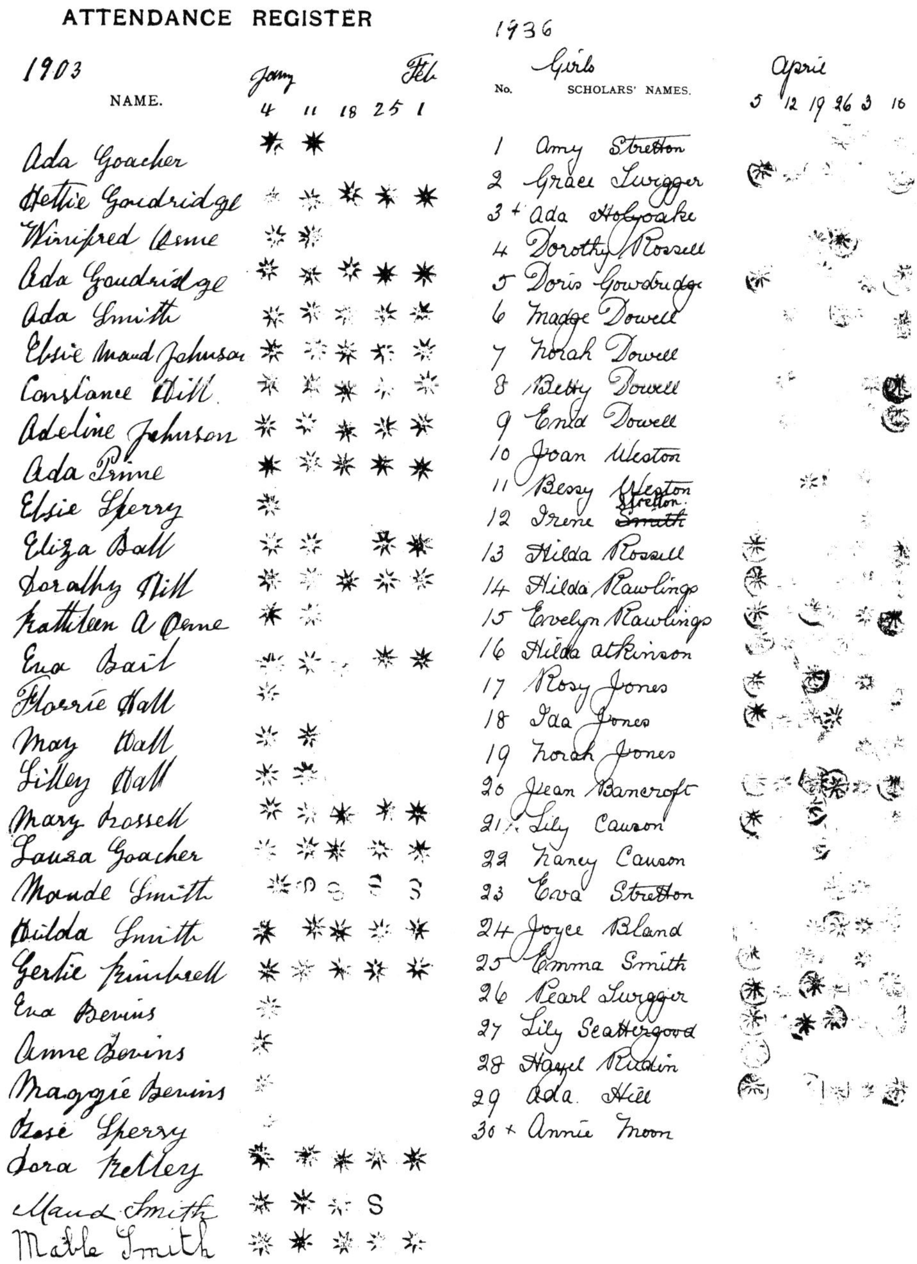

ATTENDANCE REGISTER

1903

NAME.	Jany 4	11	18	25	Feb 1
Ada Goacher	*	*			
Hettie Goodridge	*	*	*	*	*
Winifred Osme	*	*			
Ada Goodridge	*	*	*	*	*
Ada Smith	*	*	*	*	*
Elsie Maud Johnson	*	*	*	*	*
Constance Hill	*	*	*	*	*
Adeline Johnson	*	*	*	*	*
Ada Prime	*	*	*	*	*
Elsie Sperry	*				
Eliza Ball	*	*		*	*
Dorothy Hill	*	*	*	*	*
Kathleen A Osme	*	*			
Eva Bail	*	*		*	*
Florrie Hall	*				
May Hall	*	*			
Lilley Hall	*	*			
Mary Rossell	*	*	*	*	*
Laura Goacher	*	*	*	*	*
Maude Smith	*	S	S	S	S
Hilda Smith	*	*	*	*	*
Gertie Kimbrell	*	*	*	*	*
Eva Bevins	*				
Annie Bevins	*				
Maggie Bevins	*				
Rose Sperry	*				
Dora Kelley	*	*	*	*	*
Maud Smith	*	*	*	S	
Mable Smith	*	*	*	*	*

1936

Girls — April 5, 12, 19, 26, 3, 10

No.	SCHOLARS' NAMES.
1	Amy Stretton
2	Grace Swigger
3 +	Ada Holyoake
4	Dorothy Rossell
5	Doris Gowdridge
6	Madge Dowell
7	Norah Dowell
8	Betty Dowell
9	Enid Dowell
10	Joan Weston
11	Bessy Weston
12	Irene ~~Smith~~ Stretton
13	Hilda Rossell
14	Hilda Rawlings
15	Evelyn Rawlings
16	Hilda Atkinson
17	Rosy Jones
18	Ida Jones
19	Norah Jones
20	Jean Bancroft
21 x	Lily Cawson
22	Nancy Cawson
23	Eva Stretton
24	Joyce Bland
25	Emma Smith
26	Pearl Swigger
27	Lily Scattergood
28	Hazel Ridlin
29	Ada Hill
30 +	Annie Moon

Part of Girls Attendance Register Books – for years 1903 & 1936.
The stars built up towards the annual prize.

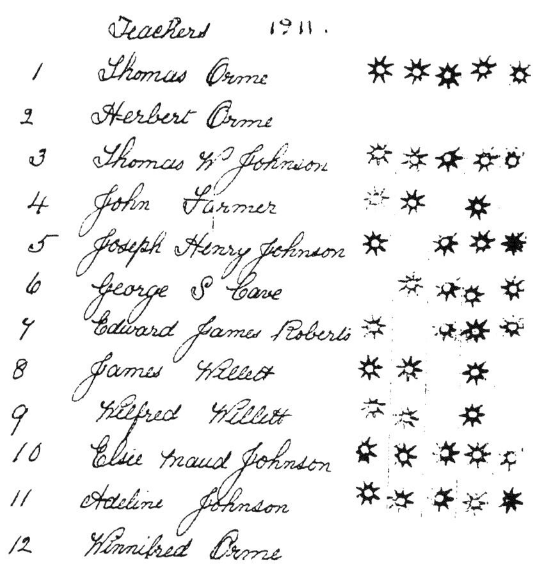
Teachers 1911.

1 Thomas Orme
2 Herbert Orme
3 Thomas W. Johnson
4 John Farmer
5 Joseph Henry Johnson
6 George S Cave
7 Edward James Roberts
8 James Willett
9 Wilfred Willett
10 Elsie Maud Johnson
11 Adeline Johnson
12 Winnifred Orme

The twelve Sunday school teachers in 1911 showing how they also earned stars on the register.

Sunday School Outings & Holidays

Another family who were good workers, and well respected members at Cross Hills, were the Walker's of Bagworth. Most Sundays during the 1920's, after the evening service, the 'young adults' would be asked to go down to Mr. and Mrs. Walker's for a 'sing song' around the piano, and supper afterwards.

For several years, Len, their son organised Cross Hills summer holidays. The first was a week at Skegness in 1921, and later to the 'Mecca' of English resorts— Blackpool! They always went to the same boarding house, number 7, Barnsley House, in Vance Road— full board for adults at five guineas per week. They travelled by train from Bagworth railway station and had their own reserved carriage. The windows of the carriage were plastered with labels bearing the words, 'Mr. WALKER'S PARTY'. No doubt the journey would be a jolly one as they 'chuffed' their way northwards.

No trip to Blackpool is complete without a visit 'up the tower', and one day several members decided to go up on the lift. When they reached the top, it was so gusty that the tower could be felt to sway in the wind. This proved to be 'too much' for the squeamish few— who promptly caught the next lift down.

Cross Hills has always been renowned for its 'lusty' singing, and everyone enjoyed helping 'Blind George', who played his concertina on the sands. Of course, one of the favourite hymns sung was 'Will your anchor hold in the storms of life'.

Here is the party posing for a photograph. Mr. and Mrs. Walker are seated in the entrance gate, and Leonard (their son) is seated on the left hand side of the photograph, behind the children. But, how many others can you name?

Cross Hills holiday party to Blackpool about 1924. The party used to help 'Blind George' who played hymn tunes for people to sing to on the sands.

'Blind George' – with his concertina.

Cross Hills Sunday school class 1905.

Deacons and members on a Sunday school outing to Abbey Park, Leicester in 1931.

Mothers on a Sunday school treat 1934.

Scholars on their Sunday school treat 1934.

Twenty-four happy Cross Hills children on a Sunday school outing in 1932.
Back row: Edna Twigger, Florence Platts, Hazel Rudin, Pearl Twigger, Joan Layton.
2nd row: Joan Smith Grace Twigger, Annie Moon, Thelma Atkins, Hilda Rawlings, Doris Gowdridge, Amy Stretton. 3rd row: Violet Shaw, Nora Dowell, Madge Dowell, Leslie Scattergood, Evelyn Rawlings, Billy Scattergood, Lily Scattergood. Front row: Irene Stretton, Ernie Scattergood, Betty Dowell, Grace Treadwell, Eva Stretton.

Sunday school outing to Alton Towers 1957.

A modern Sunday School outing in 1996 to Stoughton Farm Park, Leicester.

Mr. Harry Bancroft, aged 98, an old Sunday school scholar.

Second Service

A request was put forward by the Minister, Rev. John H. Noddings, to commence the introduction of morning service in order to bring the children into closer fellowship with the church. He said that the young folk were the 'Church of the Future', and by holding a Family Service, families, parents and children could be brought together. The first of the morning services commenced on April 1st 1973 at 10.30am, the stipulation being that each service should last no longer than one hour. This arrangement is still in existence today, 25 years later on.

CHAPTER 13

ORGANS

Sunday School Organ.... Renovation or Replacement?

The question of the thorough renovation of the organ, or even obtaining a replacement organ, was discussed on March 14th 1914. But no decision could be reached and the subject was left in abeyance for a considerable time.

It was not until the meeting of December 6th 1916 that the purchase of a secondhand organ, from Mrs. Garratt of Bagworth, was discussed. The organ, costing £14-0-0d, was designated for use of the Sunday school. Responsibility for covering the instrument when not in use, and general care, was assigned to Mr. Walter Bland, with expenses charged to the Organ Fund

New Church Organ

The question of a new organ was initially brought up by Mr Clifford Farmer on March 7th 1934. After some discussion the subject was left in abeyance until the special meeting on November 28th. It was decided to start an Organ Fund and the proceeds from the Public Tea and Lecture on July 21st 1934 should also go to the Organ Fund. A Committee was formed for the organ project, consisting of Rev. E.J. Garnham, Mr. John Farmer, Clifford Farmer, Mr. William Prime and Mrs Elsie Roberts.

It was decided to replace the little 'Harmonium' type organ, which was hardly big enough to swell the walls of the chapel and lift the hearts to the heavens. It stood in the middle of the choir beneath the petal window in the gallery. Another, bigger pipe organ was sought after, and a Mr. Bedwell, organ builder from Cambridge and Southend-on-Sea was contacted. It was known that he had recently installed one of his pipe organs at the Coalville Ebenezer Baptist Chapel.

The 'funds' were standing at a very low ebb for purchasing a new organ, and many meetings took place between the members and deacons of Cross Hills. Several letters from Mr. Bedwell and Mr. John Farmer, the Secretary, were exchanged. Quotations were given by Mr. Bedwell for two organs that he had restored, which had originated from stately homes. They were not large, as some organs are, but a suitable size at an affordable price for Cross Hills' requirements.

Mr. Bedwell was even agreeable to be paid by instalment arrangement. After the church turned down his first offer of an organ for £200 plus erection and tuning costs, he offered a second organ. This would cost £180, the erecting and tuning £27, transportation by the church was estimated at £3. The terms of hire purchase were £25 to be sent with order, £15 to be paid when organ was erected, £12 to be paid within two months. The balance of £155 to be paid within 18 months. He also made the stipulation that the responsibility of collecting the organ from Cambridge lay with the church. These terms were accepted by the organ committee.

At that time the organ lay completely dismantled in a chapel in Cambridge. The next problem was how to transport it over such a long distance (about 70 miles from Cross Hills) at an economic price.

Transportation Problem Solved

George Willett made a deal with Cross Hills church committee to transport the organ from Cambridge to Cross Hills on his lorry for £3-0s-0d.

The photograph shows George delivering coal in Buttermere Street (next to the City football ground) in 1929).

It is thought that it was on this lorry that the organ was transported from Cambridge in 1935. He set out from Bagworth early one morning, loaded up the bits and pieces, and returned the same day. In those days of more primitive engineering and unreliable axle shafts and ignition systems, this was quite a feat.

George Willett's lorry transported the organ from Cambridge to Cross Hills.

When he reached Cross Hills in the evening, the Christian Endeavour meeting had started, but was soon abandoned as everyone set to, helping George unload the precious cargo. All the bits and pieces were carefully laid out on the floor of the Sunday School, remaining there until Mr. Bedwell could come over to install the organ.

With the organ being so much bigger than its predecessor, alterations had to be made to accommodate it. Some choir seating had to be removed and a lot of carpentry work done to the gallery. Mr. Jim Gamble, a carpenter and member of Cross Hills did this work, assisted by Mr. Arch Ball.

Official Opening Day of the New Pipe Organ

Official opening of the pipe organ was arranged for Saturday February 2nd 1935, to be opened by Mr. Lloyd of Leicester. The opening ceremony was performed at 3pm, Public Tea at 4pm and Evening Service at 6.30pm. Miss Ivy Loveday of Barlestone sang at the opening.

Wind of Change ... Pipe Organ to be Fitted with Electric Blower

Mr. Bedwell, who supplied the pipe organ, sent a message that he could install an electric blower to the instrument for £50. This was accepted, and the electrical wiring for the blower was carried out by Mr. Les Hill of Newbold Verdon, December 11th 1946, after many years of hard labour 'hand blowing'!

THE CHRISTIAN ENDEAVOUR HYMNAL REVISED

(1933 Edition)

Joint Editors :

JOHN POLLOCK, D.D.

CAREY BONNER

Published for

THE CHRISTIAN ENDEAVOUR UNION OF GT. BRITAIN AND IRELAND

By the

CHRISTIAN ENDEAVOUR BOOK SALOON

4 Ave Maria Lane, Ludgate Hill, London, E.C.4

The original Christian Endeavour Hymnal was published by the newly formed British Council in 1896. This was the 1933 edition used at Cross Hills.

CHAPTER 14

ORGANISTS

Mrs Roberts: Organist for 60 Years

In May 1968 recognition was given to Mrs. Roberts for completing 60 years of loyal service as Organist, her music having emanated round the church throughout the reign of four monarchs. This magnificent achievement, members of the Church Committee heard, should be subject to some form of befitting appreciation. The proposal was that £60 be presented to her, but on March 25th it was learnt that Mrs. Roberts would accept only half the presentation money, having counted it a privilege to serve the Lord. She promptly instructed the Church to spend the other half of the money on something useful, which they did, but also Mr & Mrs Roberts were sent to Blackpool for a week's holiday.

Mrs. Elsie Roberts was a pupil of Tom Marvin and daughter of Mr. Thos. Walmsley (deacon). She was a faithful servant of the chapel, playing regularly week after week, often for both the afternoon and evening services. With half her presentation money handed back, the other half bought a new pair of oak entrance gates for the chapel. These gates still stand at the entrance to the graveyard today as a fitting tribute to Mrs Roberts' services.

Mrs. Elsie Roberts 1893 - 1979
'Organist for 60 glorious years'!

On February 26th 1968 Mrs Joyce Marriott became the new church Organist.

It should be noted that Mr Alan Brooks was elected Assistant Church Organist on April 11th 1962. On February 14th 1978 a letter was received from him, saying he needed to resign as an organist for Cross Hills after 16 years service. In reply, a letter of thanks for his services was sent to him.

The Committee also expressed thanks to Mrs. Joyce Marriott for her continuing services as Organist. Mr. T. Prime proposed on March 20th 1973 that Mrs Roberts should be appointed Honorary Organist in view of her many years of faithful service.

Mrs. Roberts died on August 2nd 1979 aged 86 years, and is aptly buried in the graveyard of the chapel she so much loved and laboured for. 'Well done thou good and faithful servant'

CHAPTER 15

CHRISTIAN ENDEAVOUR

The Christian Endeavour movement was interdenominational, which began in America and came to Great Britain in the 1890's. It's motto was, 'For Christ & the Church'. Members wore a C.E. badge on their lapel as illustrated above— see also photograph of E.J. Garnham on page 93.

The object of Christian Endeavour was to reach, hold, instruct, train and inspire young people for consecrated Christian living, Service and Church leadership.

A British Christian Endeavour Union was formed, which was subdivided into areas. Cross Hills Baptist Church became affiliated before 1910 and became part of the Leicestershire and North Warwickshire Federation, which incorporated Leicester, Hinckley, Coventry and Nuneaton Unions.

Meetings were held weekly at Cross Hills, mainly in the winter months in a small room at the rear of the chapel. This room was known as the Christian Endeavour Room.

On a wall, in a picture frame, was the following covenant which the members would read aloud:

The Christian Endeavour Covenant

> Relying on the Lord, Jesus Christ, for salvation and trusting in God for strength, I promise Him that I will strive to do whatever He would like to have me do; I will pray to Him and read the Bible everyday, I will support my own church and its services in every way within my power, and throughout my whole life I will endeavour to lead a Christian life.

There was also a junior C.E. which was well attended. Not only Cross Hills children and youth joined, but members from the Church of England also attended.

Each year a 'President' was appointed to lead the meetings and speak on a 'topic' prepared by the British C.E. Union. The meeting was then thrown 'open' for any member to speak. From these humble beginnings, through taking part, many members became adept at speaking at these meetings, some progressing to become Lay Preachers, Ministers of the Church, and even missionaries. Whilst others had the honour of becoming 'Presidents' of the Leicester & District C.E. Union.

Christian Endeavour Anniversary weekends were held each September, when special speakers were invited from various parts of the country to deliver an address. During these occasions, good times of fellowship were experienced among members. It was therefore very unfortunate when the meetings grew less and less at Cross Hills, until we came to the stage that this branch of C.E. no longer existed and has never revived since, to the detriment of the church.

The above account of Cross Hills Christian Endeavour was supplied by Mr. George Farmer, Life Deacon of Cross Hills and former member of the Christian Endeavour.

CHAPTER 16

CARETAKERS AND REPAIRS TO PROPERTY

Repairs, Renovation and Funding

With a view to raising funds to cover the cost of repairing damaged church property and the painting of the chapel, it was proposed to organise a garden party on Wednesday August 29th 1923. The event was to be held in a field belonging to Mr. C. Massey, of Thornton.

'Reservoir Farm' Thornton, home of Mr. & Mrs. Charles Massey.

Mr. Massey proposed engaging a band, for which tenders would be sent to both Bagworth and Thornton bands. Admission for adults was set at 6d, including tax; children 3d. Unfavourable weather proved a stumbling block when the garden party day arrived. After paying all expenses, a profit of £4-15s-6d was in hand for the Renovation Fund.

Undeterred by the inclement weather, it was decided to hold a second garden party. Mr. and Mrs. P.J. Hill of Bagworth threw open their farm for this purpose, the profit this time for the Renovation Fund resulted in £11-10s-61/2d being raised.

Renovation Account

Estimated costs for renovating the church throughout resulted in the lowest tender for the painting being awarded to Mr. E.J. Wheatley. He estimated the work would take him a month, and was less than half the price of the highest tender. The work started on June 6th 1932, and in conjunction with other tradesmen, the costs were as follows:

Mr. Wheatley		£87-8s-0d
Mr. R. Blower		£40-6s-10d
Mr. F. Lawrence		£9-18s-7d
Mr. & Mrs. Weston, Caretakers		£1-10s-0d
	Total	£139-3s-5d

Everyone in the Church was very pleased that the whole cost of the project had been paid out of the Renovation Account. The Treasurer, Mr. Wm. Prime reported they had a balance in hand in the Renovation Account of £2-0s-0d and for the Church, a balance of £4-12s-8d.

CHURCH SERVICES – OF THE ELECTRICAL, WATER AND HEATING VARIETY!

Desford Colliery Coal

Three tons of coal were ordered from Desford colliery at 9/- per ton, on the 27th of September 1910. Note that Desford Mine was only nine years old at the time.

Christopher Lawrence Legacy for Lighting and Heating

Mr. H. Orme and Mr J.T. Lawrence attended the April 7th meeting, 1915, as Trustees of the late Mr. Christopher Lawrence, who had left a legacy of £100 for the church's investment. The legacy was to be invested in National War Bonds. On April 10th 1919 it was passed at the church meeting that Mr. Charles Massey and Mr.

John Thomas Lawrence - Thornton tailor whose father Mr Christopher Lawrence left a legacy to the chapel, also Thornton school clock, which is still 'Going Strong'.

Herbert Orme would act as Trustees for the investment. The interest accrued was to be used for the purpose of heating and lighting Cross Hills property and is still in existence today.

Boiler Replacement: Subscription List to Pay the Bill

Rev. E.J. Garnham was advised, on September 14th 1927 to write to Messenger & Co., Loughborough, asking them to come over and examine the furnace and boiler. The Church required to know whether the equipment could be repaired, or needed replacing.

At this meeting, Mr. Reginald Willett was granted permission to supply coal and wood for the furnace. He explained that his brother, George, had started up in the coal delivery trade, so the Committee decided to give them the contract provided the coal was of a suitable type.

It was found, on October 5th 1927, that a new boiler and furnace were required, costing £30-10s-0d. Oliver Dilks was engaged to do the brickwork; Reg Willett and Len Walker were mustered to open a Subscription List *'...to see what money we could get for the new boiler'*. This was an extra source to the money raised by the Renovation Fund.

New Oil Lamps For Old

Mr. Walmsley proposed and Mr. Len Walker seconded that new lamps were to be purchased for the Church. The lamps referred to were oil lamps, similar to the ones which can be seen in the photograph.

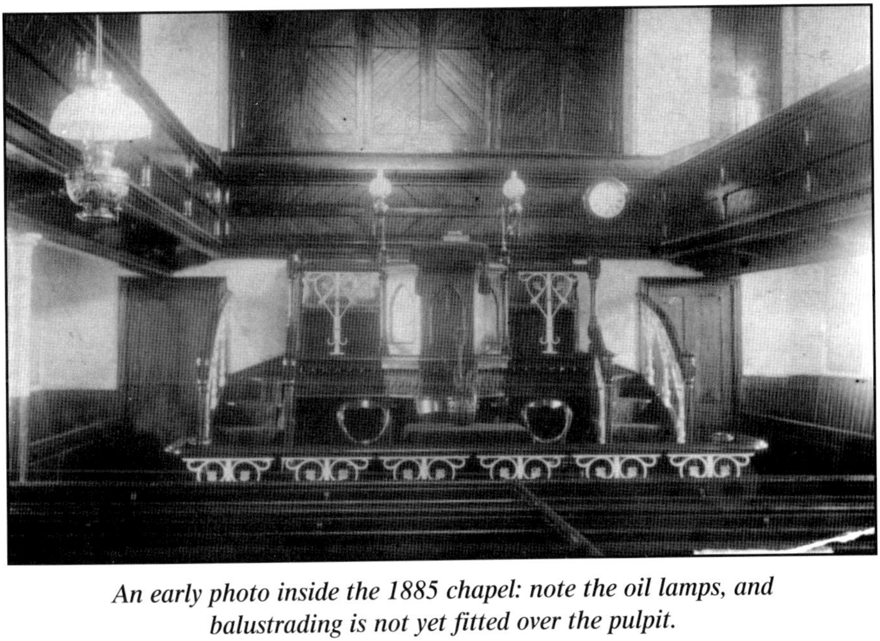

An early photo inside the 1885 chapel: note the oil lamps, and balustrading is not yet fitted over the pulpit.

On March 16th 1932 came the first indication of mains electricity being laid for the church buildings. Rev. E.J. Garnham wrote to Mr. Thursfield of Hinckley to find out whether it was possible to get mains power to the chapel for the purpose of electric lighting installation.

Mr Thursfield wrote back with an estimate of £82, which was more than was expected, and over what the church was prepared to pay. So it seems, the Friends of the church thought that electric lighting was overrated, and vowed they would 'keep on with the oil lamps.' At least until the price was acceptable.

Electric Lighting Reaches Cross Hills at Last

Tenders were sent out to six electrical installation firms to install electric lights in the chapel. On September 30th 1937 Mr. Kemp of Coalville was favoured with an estimate of £35-12s-0d. It was resolved to write to Mr. Kemp and get the wiring and fittings put in as soon as possible. Thoughts now centred on finding some suitable person to officially switch on the lights in the near future, but it is not clear who was engaged.

REAL-LIFE STORY No. 1

Mr. Annis's Protracted Lecture

Mr. Cecil Annis of Thornton offered on October 10th 1923 to lecture on *'The Life of Charles Dickens'*, which was accepted by the Committee and the arrangements made.

The lecture was well attended and Mr. Garnham presided. Crammed full of Charles Dickens' books for the occasion, the legs of the baptistry table fair buckled. As the lecture proceeded, each book was laboriously referred to by the speaker. At last, the final book was put down, much to the relief of his weary audience, who were mainly unused to the 'heavy classical stuff'.

Just then, the puffing of the 9.40pm steam train from Leicester through Bagworth only emphasized how late it was to the audience, and prompted the signal for stifled yawns. But to the dismay of many, Cecil fetched in yet another stack of books from the vestry. As a general groan went round, one member of the congregation saw fit to see 'the funny side of it all', his laughter fairly shaking the pew.

Mr. Garnham, who had apparently also had 'had enough' of Dickens for one night, bravely jumped up and said tactfully, 'Well, thank you so much Mr. Annis for a very informative lecture— perhaps we can hear about the other books another time.' Much to the huge relief of everyone!

Caretaker Extraordinary

An interesting letter, written to Mr. H.J. Cooper upon his appointment as Caretaker of Cross Hills, is reproduced below in full. It illustrates the high responsibility placed on lowly casual workers, and the remuneration they earned.

Bagworth Baptist Chapel,

February 11th 1929.

The Deacons of the above Church hereby appoint Mr. Cooper of Thornton as Caretaker of the above Church, whose duties are as follows:

1) To light the furnace fire and to see that there is plenty of water pumped into the tank. Also to see that there is no air in pipes. Furnace fire to be lit every day during frosty weather, and every weekend during cold weather so that School Room and Chapel be comfortable for services.

2) Sunday School: to open doors at 9.30am - 1.30pm.

Chapel Sunday services: doors to be opened at 1.45pm and at 5.45pm. All lamps to be lit suitable for those services.

3) Week Night Services: Wednesday, To open doors, light fire in classroom and light lamps for Service at 7.30pm. Also, to open doors and light fire and lamps at any meeting that shall be called.

4) To light and to keep clean all lamps. Also, to see that all lamps are kept full of oil for evening services.

5) To see that all windows and doors are closed and locked. Also, that all lights are put out after services.

6) To keep clean all graveyard paths, also hedge around graveyard, and to mow graveyard when required.

7) All duties to be performed to the satisfaction of the Deacons.

8) That three months notice be given by either party to give up above named duties.

Remuneration for above named duties to be paid at the rate of £5-0-0 per year to be paid quarterly at £1-5s-0d a quarter.

signed on behalf of the Deacons.

John Farmer, Secretary.

signed, Mr. H.J. Cooper.

(Caretaker's signature binding the contract)

SUNDAY SCHOOL

PRAISE

NATIONAL SUNDAY SCHOOL UNION
104-5 NEWGATE STREET, LONDON, E.C.1

The Sunday School Hymn book which was used extensively in the 'early days' and founded in 1803.

CHAPTER 17

BAPTISMS AND MORE REAL LIFE STORIES

Baptisms

Baptisms were a regular occurrence at Cross Hills, and a fine example of this was apparent at the Baptismal Service on Thursday June 18th 1931, when no fewer than eleven candidates were baptised. Pastor R.D. Browne officiated at the ceremony, which included Mr. and Mrs. Nicklin of Leicester. They had expressed their desire to be baptised at Bagworth at the same session as the other nine candidates. Permission was sought from the General Church, at this time, to buy extra Baptismal Gowns for both ladies and gents.

Baptismal Service of Young People

A meeting was called to ask the acceptance into the church of candidates nominated for Baptism on December 8th 1951. The candidates were, Miss Joyce Prime, Miss Rhoda Hollyoak, Miss Joyce Whitmore, (later to become a Missionary) and others from Newbold Verdon.

A Baptismal Service was conducted by the Rev. Peter Peel at Cross Hills Church on May 22nd 1965 on Saturday evening at 7pm. The following young people were baptised: Glynis Watkins, Delsya Bateman, Susan Squires, Mary Farmer, Colin Harris and Alan Brooks. The young people were received into Membership on Sunday May 23rd.

It was with much pleasure on April 21st 1968 that Cross Hills Church accepted for membership by baptism, Mrs. M. Whitmore and Mrs. Rene Watkins. The Baptismal Service was integrated into the afternoon service, while the nominees were formally received into Fellowship at the evening Communion Service.

Technical details recorded in the book of minutes: the Minister arranged for his own equipment and for the hiring of the Baptismal Heater; Mrs Harris organised, with the ladies concerned, all the Baptismal Gowns; Mr. Brooks tested the Baptistry to ensure that it was in order and water tight.

Trees Are Conkered

The date was March 20th in darkest 1940, deep in the throws of World War II. There was a report that not only were we susceptible to air attacks, but by local children who were hurling sticks at the horse chestnut trees in the graveyard for the purpose of procuring conkers.

No doubt the church windows were at risk with flying missiles, which was one reason why the Church officials contemplated cutting the trees— it is not clear to what extent they actually went. Also, many graves had artificial flowers covered by glass domes at this period, and these were getting broken.

This drastic tree-felling measure was deferred for another year to find out if warning notices had any effect in deterring the culprits. The cutting down of trees is always a drastic measure. And when those trees happen to be horse chestnuts, some children, and many fathers, find it particularly traumatic at the loss of their supply of conkers. But at Cross Hills it eventually became imperative when water, dripping from the overhead canopy of leaves in the graveyard, were found to be seriously damaging the memorial stones.

For the last ten years the trees had been enjoying a reprieve from 'execution', but their time was now sadly running out. A suggestion was made on January 18th 1950 to cut down the offending trees. Mr. Ray Screaton, of Bagworth, was approached to engage him in removing the 'conker trees' with the stipulation that he accepts the timber in lieu of payment.

REAL-LIFE STORY No 2

A Woody Story

Straight across the road from Cross Hills in the hedge stands a massive ash tree. With its huge branches towering heavenwards it has overshadowed the chapel for many years. This provided an ideal home for the many raucous rooks that built their nests each spring in the treetop, accompanied by much noise and mess.

The ash tree and the nests seemed to pose a challenge to local boys.

One of the more dubious hobbies of local boys years ago was egg collecting. Unlike many varieties of wild birds, the rooks' nests are never concealed, although very inaccessible. The rooks doubtless sensed that they were safe from predators— but they were not taking into account the ambitions of one or two Cross Hills tearaways during the 1940's. They definitely had a head for heights, although one of the main problems was climbing the first section— the first 10 feet of trunk was unsociably smooth and slippery. Something had to be found to overcome this problem.

The wayward lads did not have far to look. Straight across the road were the ornate iron gates in front of the main entrance of the church, and the still existing double gates into the graveyard. Along the top edge of the gates were a row of sharp metal spikes. Some of these were broken off and hammered into the bole of the tree to form footholds, much to the dismay of the rooks.

The absence of four spikes from the top of the gate is still conspicuous today. But at least, for the past 50 years, any rooks inhabiting the tree have lived in peace!

True Cross Hills Humour

Two old deacons walking up the hill to Bagworth after a rather 'dry' sermon:

John — 'I didn't think much to the speaker broadcasting the sermon tonight, Tom.'

Tom — 'There was nowt the matter with the speaker, it was the receiving end that weren't tuned in!'

Celebrating 50th Anniversary of 1885 Church Opening.
Left to Right: Rev. Garnham, L. Walker, Wm. Prime, John Farmer, Herbert Orme, Thos. Walmsley, Reuben Blower, Chas. Massey, Sir William Edge M.P.

50th Jubilee

A Garden Party was to be arranged at the Church meeting of Wednesday March 20th 1935 when no fewer than 32 people were recruited to form the garden party committee.

Mr. H. Orme reminded the meeting that it would be 50 years in July 1935 since foundation stones were laid for the building of the chapel. It was decided to arrange some special services to commemorate the event. Sir William Edge, M.P. was procured to take the Chair at the afternoon Jubilee celebrations, on November 2nd 1935 at 3pm,. The Rev. E.J. Garnham gave a brief account of the history of Cross Hills Church. This was followed by a public tea at 5pm, with all proceeds earmarked for the Organ Fund.

Reginald Willett's Wife Emma, Remembered

Mr. Reginald Willett sought and procured permission from the church meeting to allow the group, 'Young Life Campaign' to have the use of the chapel and schoolroom on Saturday May 4th 1935. Mr. Willett donated three oak chairs for the 'Baptistry' in memory of his wife, Mrs. Emma Willett, who died on February 5th 1936. The chairs, which are still in use, were made by Mr. Burditt of Ibstock.

Sankey Hymn Books

The decision was taken on March 17th 1942 to purchase 25 large and 50 small Sankeys Hymn books for regular use at the Sunday evening service. The books were to be bought through Mr. J.A. Nicklin, of Leicester.

New Gates for Old

At a meeting on June 2nd 1960, it was suggested that a new pair of entrance gates should be purchased for the front and side entrance to the church, and the old gates resited at the rear of the Sunday school. This was an improvement which had for some time been considered, since the original gates were broken.

A small gate was also erected on the corner of the Sunday school, near the graveyard in June 1961.

Amenity Extension

February 28th 1962 saw the builder, Mr. C.J. Haughton of Bagworth, win with his estimate to construct toilets and kitchen for the church.

The total cost of the project, which included an insulated slate roof, was £364-12s-0d.

Seat of the Problem

All the old bench-type wooden seats from the Sunday school had been removed and disposed of by October 20th 1966 and had been replaced by canvas and steel chairs. Forty eight new chairs had been bought, with the option to purchase more as required.

PART V: CROSS HILLS GOES WORLDWIDE

CHAPTER 18

MISSIONARIES

On June 28th 1933 it was proposed that 'we have a Mission, to commence on October 15th.' The Mission took place over a period of two weeks, conducted by Mr.H. Careless, who used to travel around in a caravan as an evangelical preacher. Some farmer's field would be the venue to pitch his large tent, inside which he would conduct his services, having only the thickness of canvas cloth separating his flock from the heavens. This was particularly pleasing in the summer time, and often Mr. Careless's tent would be full for both the adult and the children's services.

Cross Hills was pleased to procure the services of Mr. R.W. Jones, of the 'Caravan Mission to Village Children', as the preacher for the 1952 Anniversary Service.

This letter was sent by Mr. Ken Smith to Cross Hills, from the Baptist Training Institute, Glasgow, on May 28th 1947.

My dear friends,

Greetings in the name of our Lord Jesus Christ. It is with deep thankfulness of heart that I endeavour to write and express these thanks.

I am very grateful for your love and unity manifested in your very kind gift of £25.

I pray God may richly bless in this work, that we may endeavour under his guidance to do.

There is but one mission field, and that the world (John 4:35). Whether at home or abroad, we who follow the Saviour, we who are blood bought are sent forth by him to witness and show forth the love of God, the way of life.

I greatly value your prayers in my going forth and in my labours. I often remember you all before the throne of grace, giving thanks every remembrance, the early years in the Sunday School and the junior Christian Endeavour, the training of the Christian Endeavour, and the years in the Church, especially since it was in the School Room of Cross Hills where I first met my Lord as Saviour, Redeemer and King.

I feel the news of yesterday will be of interest to you all. It was the closing day of the 49th British C.E. convention, the morning meeting was the missionary rally which was attended by some 500. Dr. A. Taylor, of China was the speaker.

I was greatly privileged to take an active part. Four missionaries were to give testimonies. Two on Africa, one on China, and I represented India.

I also met Mr. Sharpe of Coventry who was very interested in my going forth, and took particulars to register it at Head Quarters as an Endeavourer from Cross Hills out in the foreign field.

God's richest blessings be yours.

Very many thanks

Yours ever in Calvary's Bonds

Ken W. Smith.

Hebrews 4: 12: 16

Letter from Mrs Bee Smith, wife of Ken Smith (both missionaries to India for 40 years.)

Ken and I met at B.T.I. Glasgow. I went out to India October 1946 and Ken followed a year after, and we were married the following January. We lived first of all in a village of Bihar. While learning the language we did some medical work as there were few doctors then, and also visited the many villages around. We were there ten years and our son David was born.

During this time we, with other missionaries, took tents and camped in some of the distant villages. Travelling was slow by bullock cart, but Ken built a small cart and we managed to get a small pony. After a while, Ken got a large motor bike, so with me on the back, David on the petrol tank and luggage on the carrier behind, we travelled many miles.

Later on we managed to get a small car. David was then six years old and had to go to school on a hill station, which was a four days journey. We only saw him twice a year.

There was a small group of Bengali Christians about two miles from us, and we went there each Sunday. Ken did a lot of Bible teaching and during the week I had meetings for the women and girls.

At this time we were interested in the Emmaus Bible studies. These were aids to study the Bible and we sent them out by post. We had many writing to us from Calcutta, so we felt the Lord would have us move there.

A city of 12 million people and a million living on the streets. It was a tremendous contrast for us, it was difficult to find a place to live and expenses increased. The Lord never failed.

The first place we got, the mosquitoes were so bad and gave us no rest. The Baptist Mission manse was empty at that time and they asked us to live there, which we did for some months. We also got a room in the Church of Scotland and we made that our office.

Gradually we had a large number of people contacting us for the Bible studies, so on Sundays we started a meeting for them in a room at the Y.M.C.A. For some time only one came, but as we got to know them, mostly younger men, numbers increased and we had over 300 at our quarterly meeting.

A team of young people from America came out to help us for three months and in that time we sold many thousands of gospels on the street, and each gospel had a bible study in it. We had many requests for further Bible studies and many students came to see us.

One young man bought a gospel thinking it was communist literature, and was training to be a Hindu priest. He came to see us many times and listened to the Word. He was wonderfully converted, suffered much persecution, but after years of listening he joined us in the work and now carries on after we left.

Mr Ken Smith and his wife, Mrs Bee Smith, missionaries to India for 40 years.

After some time we were able to rent a big house and grounds from the Baptist Mission and gradually folks got to know us, and we were able to have camps for students, children, girls and elderly women. Each group came for a week at a time. We had various games for them, table tennis, badminton, sewing for the girls and toys for the children. Twice a day there was Bible teaching. For these dear people to get a good meal twice a day, a good bed and plenty of water to wash in, it meant a lot.

Each one who finished three of our Bible courses received a New Testament and a certificate which we gave out at a special meeting for them. In this way, we contacted some of the Upper classes as well as the very poor. A number were converted, but because of severe persecution, were afraid to confess the Lord openly.

I also helped in an old people's home, and we had them to tea in the garden. During these years we experienced flood, earth tremors, riots, and day to day dependence on the Lord for finance. He never failed us.

Altogether we were in India for 40 years and always have so much to praise the Lord for.

Bee Smith

The following account has been written by Miss Joyce Whitmore—Cross Hills Sunday school Scholar; Member of the Church; Missionary to the Congo, in Africa; and the Comores Islands in the Indian Ocean; and now at the A.I.M. office in Bristol.

Miss Joyce Whitmore, Missionary

I can't remember a time when Cross Hills Baptist Church was not part of my life. (I wonder just how many times I walked along that narrow lane between Bagworth and the church!) I can remember a time when the idea of myself as a Christian Missionary was definitely not part of my thinking. As a teenager I decided that I would follow the Lord Jesus Christ, but I had no idea that faithfulness to Him would lead me halfway round the world.

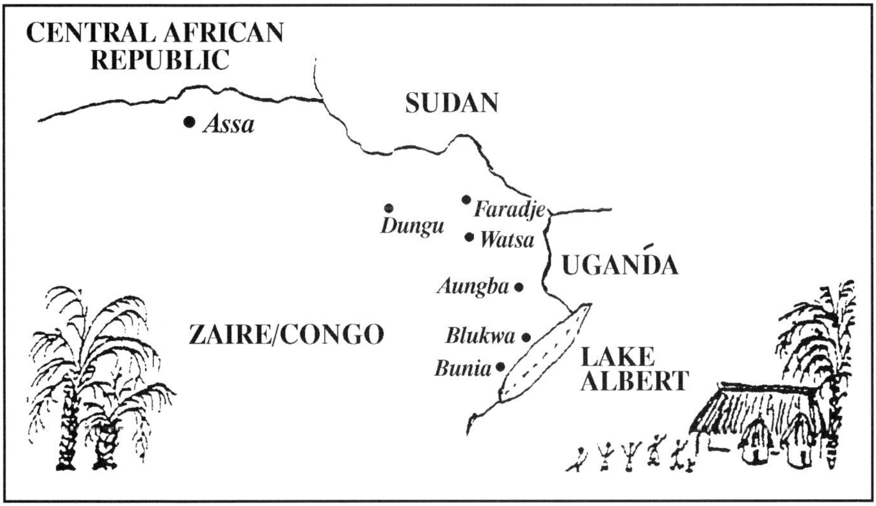

1968-1981 After a few months in Kenya I was able to take up my assignment with Africa Inland Mission as a missionary teacher in Aungba, North-Eastern Congo at the only church/mission secondary school that offered a full secondary education at the time. What a privilege to help to train many of the men who are now leaders of a church numbering tens of thousands of believers! I went to Aungba as a French teacher, but I also taught English, History and R.E. and later, at Blukwa (a school specialising in languages and the arts), Latin too.

The most satisfying part of my assignment was my involvement with the 'Christian Union in Schools' movement which began during my time there and is still active today. During those thirteen years I had a part in offering both academic and spiritual training to eleven generations of students. A Christian teacher could not ask for more, particularly as many of them are today men and women living for God in very difficult circumstances.

1982-1990 I left Congo (then Zaïre), not that I was unhappy but because God changed my direction. There were opportunities for English teachers in the Comores, a small, French-speaking, Muslim group of tropical islands just north of Madagascar in the Indian Ocean. The door was wide open, even for Christians, though in the eyes of the Government we were their servants and not missionaries. In fact we were forbidden to speak of our faith to the Comorians, unless one of them approached us. Nor could they come to the Protestant church on our island, or attend any other Christian meeting.

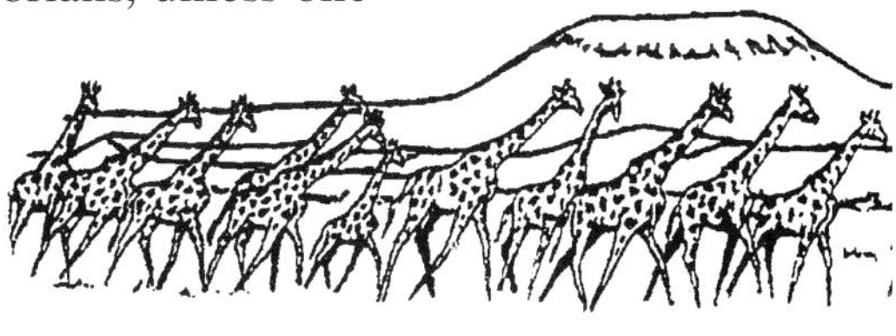

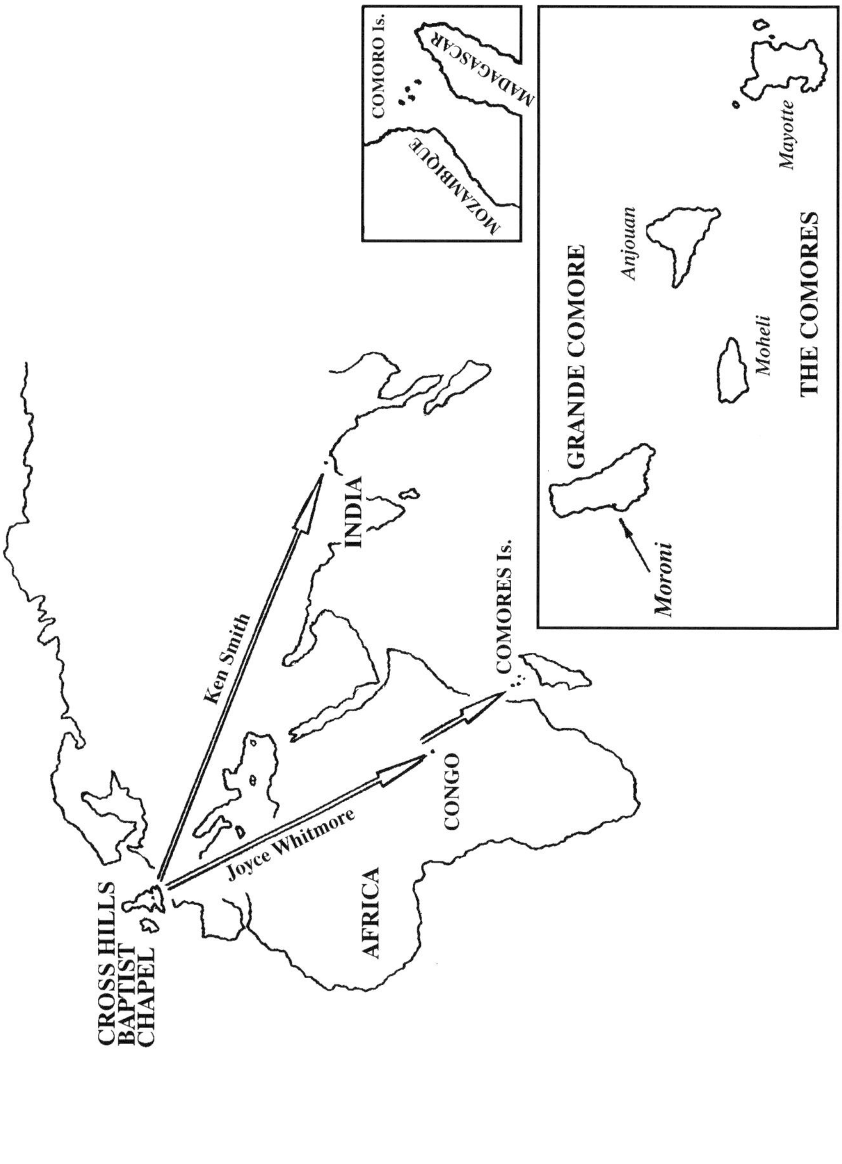
CROSS HILLS BAPTIST CHAPEL
Ken Smith
INDIA
Joyce Whitmore
CONGO
AFRICA
COMORES Is.
COMORO Is.
MADAGASCAR
MOZAMBIQUE
GRANDE COMORE
Moroni
Moheli
Anjouan
Mayotte
THE COMORES

What our students could do was come to the home that my friend Shirley and I shared and chat with us on our balcony (with its idyllic views over the ocean) and even see on the video in our lounge the visual presentation of Luke's Gospel offered by the 'Jesus' film.

Results were not spectacular, to say the least— just one young man who professed conversion and today we have lost touch with him, since he left for France like so many of his peers. This was a very different kind of missionary work, that of sowing the seeds of the Gospel in hard places and trusting God to bring a harvest in His time.

1990 to the present day Another complete change of direction! The moment had come to be nearer home and share with my sister the increasing care that our mother required. At this point I received an invitation to work in A.I.M.'s International Office in Bristol. My title is 'Administrator', my duties are many: 'servicing' the Finance Committee, ordering supplies, translating into French a quarterly 'paper' to bring instruction and encouragement to pastors deprived of reference books, proof-reading and praying with my colleagues for the work of A.I.M.... It's a great privilege to work at the very hub of the Mission's work.

Joyce Whitmore

MISSIONARIES' HOME-COMING

Return of Joyce Whitmore and Ken Smith

On November 29th, 1952 Mr. Ken Smith, back home as a Missionary in India, gave a talk and film show on his work abroad. Nineteen years on, Ken was still doing good work abroad, and on August 24th 1971, we were blessed, this time, with the home-coming of two local Missionaries. Cross Hills had much pleasure in preparing a very warm welcome for them both. Miss Joyce Whitmore was home on her first furlough from 'Aungba' (Congo and Zaire), and Mr. Ken Smith was again back from India. On October 1st, a United Missionary Meeting was held, when Joyce and Ken spoke of their work abroad, graphically illustrating their unique events with the help of film slides.

This Hymn book was originally compiled to enable the uniting power of music to operate during and after 'Mission England', in the 1980's. Many modern hymns and tunes were incorporated.

CHAPTER 19

MISCELLANEOUS STORIES:

Water & Fire Wedding

The wedding took place, in 1960, of Miss Joyce Prime, Baptist and Mr Ivan Marriott, Methodist. When Joyce and Ivan were married, it could be said that the Union of the Baptist, (water) and Methodist (fire) made very good 'steam'!

Cross Hills advice to them both was displayed on the noticeboard over Ivan's shoulder. It reads:

'whatsoever ye do, do it heartily!'

A typical Cross Hills wedding. Miss Joyce Prime & Mr Ivan Marriott.

New Car Park Constructed

The purchase of land for a car park adjoining the side of the church finally met with success when the transaction was recorded in the minutes of July 26th 1961. Mr. R. Brown of Thornton had consented to the sale of a piece of land at two shillings per square yard. The proviso attached to the sale being that the Church paid all incurred legal charges. Planning Permission for the park had been granted earlier. On April 11th 1962 Les Brooks and other members erected a fence that Les had made, at the back of the car park on the newly acquired ground.

Anglican Connection

Arrangements were disclosed, on February 24th 1970 that St. Peter's and Holy Rood churches were to stage a pageant to celebrate 750 years since the institution of their first vicar of the parish. The current vicar, Rev. J. Seymour, invited Cross Hills to take part in the pageant and produce a small sketch entitled: 'The Opening of the Chapels' , which they did.

Link Up

At the Cross Hills meeting of November 13th 1973 it was learned that the Inter Church Committee had long wanted a joint magazine for the two villages. The vicar had readily welcomed this, and commencing January 1974 the magazine would be circulated throughout Thornton and Bagworth. The publication would retain its original title of 'Parish Magazine' until January 1975, when it would henceforth be aptly called 'The Link'

REAL-LIFE STORY No. 3
WILLIAM PRIME

When William Prime Found One Bigger Than He Bargained For.

When the choirmaster, William Prime, retired from his employment as a deputy at Bagworth colliery in 1933, to maintain his fitness he would walk to Cross Hills most days. He was a deacon there, and he took it on himself to see that everything was all right and do odd jobs.

One of these odd jobs was to empty and reset the mouse traps that were placed strategically inside the chapel. The mice had no trouble getting into the church from the fields around, and could do quite a lot of damage.

They were quite partial to hymn books, sheets of music, and they even nibbled at the leather bellows on the pipe organ causing a loss of power. The felt pads on the piano striking hammers were also a delicacy. Of course, mouse droppings were to be seen everywhere!

There is an old saying: 'as poor as a church mouse', but Cross Hills mice were not poor. In fact they were large, fat and quite obese! Indeed, everything that was not made of metal, stone or brick was classed as food to the mice, as they strove to quell their voracious appetites.

They streamed into the church mainly in the winter when there was no corn in the fields. But they had to be caught— and this is where the deft hands of William came into their own.

A bizarre sight met William one day as he went on his safari rounds, and reached the antiquated toilets which were situated in outbuildings in those days. Up until the 1950's the toilets were very crude affairs with wooden seats and drop down covered lids with an ash pit underneath— there were no water toilets available at this time.

One day, William entered the gents toilet and received a very nasty shock— a huge live rat was completely caught with the thick part of its tail fast between the seat and the heavy lid, which had fallen down and trapped the unfortunate animal.

William quickly recovered, armed himself with a rusty old dustpan (not his conducting stick, as was envisioned by one fellow) and despatched the rodent to a higher plane. But what a surprise it must have been!

William Prime Calls it a Day

On June 28th 1950 eighty three year old Mr. William Prime resigned from both the Office of Treasurer for the last 42 years, and that of Choirmaster for 20 years. All present at the meeting agreed that the long service of Mr. Prime had been a most magnificent achievement and all felt that this should be marked by some kind of Testimonial. It was therefore proposed to open a subscription list among Friends to purchase retirement gifts for other Committee members, too.

Mr. Clifford Farmer was considered the most likely candidate to take over the vacant post of Choirmaster, as he possessed the necessary qualifications for this important Office. And it was '...with joyful thought...' that Mr. Tom Prime was to take over the Treasurer's job from his father, Mr. William Prime, and so carry on the tradition in the family.

A 'Meat Tea' and social evening was arranged for September 2nd 1950. Small token gifts were presented to three retiring members to recognise their remarkable service, and to recognise the high esteem and appreciation the Church held for Mr. William Prime, Choirmaster and Treasurer; Mr. J. Farmer, Secretary; and Mrs. Roberts, Organist.

Time for a Coronation Clock

On September 9th 1953 it was decided to purchase a coronation gift clock, together with a brass plaque, which reads:

> **This clock was presented to**
> **The Cross Hills Baptist Church**
> **By the Bagworth Coronation Committee**
> **to Commemorate the Coronation of**
> **H.M. QUEEN ELIZABETH II**
> **June 2nd 1953**
> **Dedicated by Rev. E.J. Garnham**
> **Nov 29th 1953**

The clock was kept in working order until about 1990, when it became too expensive to repair.

New Furniture

Mr. Les Brooks, a Deacon of Cross Hills, installed new side seats down each aisle of the chapel, in 1955. He said he required no payment for this work, as it was done to mark the appreciation for the '... hospitality shown to his family'.

Mr Les Brooks, Choirmaster.

REAL-LIFE STORY No. 4
GEORGE WILLETT— DEACON.

The Story of George and the Wagon

In 1927 after the 'General Strike' of 1926, George returned to work at Nailstone Colliery as a pony driver. He had not been back long when he and his pony were 'buried' by a fall of roof. George always maintained that the pony 'saved' him because the pony's body acted as a shield as he lay underneath it.

However, the frightening experience unnerved George to the extent that he never worked down the pit again.

George's brother, Reg, another member of Cross Hills church, owned several lorries, and he set George up with a vehicle to start a coal and haulage business. The lorry was an old Ford 'T' one ton model.

George's Crisis No. 1

George had never driven before, but undaunted he jumped in the cab and was instructed in the art of driving by his brother. Reg told him how to start and off he went, just like the 'Keystone Cops'. When he reached the 'Maynard Arms' public house he suddenly realised Reg had not told him how to stop the thing, and he really had not a clue.

He reached the Bagworth Brickyard in double quick time, and upon spotting a huge pile of ashes in the brickyard he saw this as a desperate means of stopping the rogue lorry's progress. In what could aptly be described as a very 'unconventional' manner of bringing the lorry to a halt, George aimed it straight at the ashes and the crisis was over!

George's Crisis No. 2

Another incident involving George's driving occurred up 'Ellistown Hill' when he was driving to work in the dark, one nasty and very early winter's morning.

A man was leading his pair of horses up the hill without any lights to warn others of their presence. On the darkened scene comes George in his lorry, complete with lights, albeit not very bright. Not spotting the horses in the darkness, George hit them fair and square up the backside, knocking them into the ditch.

On this occasion he was not summoned by law and escaped scot free, but on another occasion was not so lucky. George had bought a new lorry from Paynes of Hinckley and was proudly driving his new acquisition home on the night of 'Bagworth Wakes'. This was in the days when vehicle lighting was in the form of paraffin lamps that were fitted as side lights. Throngs of people filled the streets at this special time and especially around the entrance to the fairground in Barlestone Road.

Among the crowd were two policemen dutifully keeping Law and Order. George was flagged down to a halt, which left him bewildered to know how he had blighted the Law. He soon learned that, unbeknown to him, one of his paraffin sidelights had been shaken out of action when his lorry bounced over a pothole.

Much to George's disapproval at being nobbled for such a trivial offence, he was summoned and fined for only having one sidelight.

CHAPTER 20

EVENTS IN THE CHRISTIAN CALENDAR

EASTER

Meetings at Easter were always arranged by 'the group' of Baptist churches, and held in each chapel in turn. In addition to Cross Hills own Easter services, conducted by the local Minister or Pastor, a special speaker was invited to preach.

HARVEST FESTIVALS

Harvest Thanksgiving Services

Wonderful times for celebration have always been the Harvest Thanksgiving Services. Great efforts were made to bring produce to church, to thank God for his wonderful gifts. Everywhere in the church was decorated with flowers, fruits, vegetables, corn, eggs, and indeed all the produce you can name.

Farmers particularly, are grateful for a good harvest and before 'combine harvesters', would supply Cross Hills with sheaves of corn which were always placed one at each end of the baptistry.

The table on the baptistry was three-tiered and covered with a white table cloth. All the produce was arranged from the baptistry up to the pulpit, with the usual glass of water and lump of coal in the middle.

The front of the galleries were decorated with branches from apple trees with the fruit still attached. Window cills were full of flowers, fruit and vegetables of every variety and colour.

Some members who were keen and talented at displaying at horticultural shows were very active at this time. Winston Jones of Thornton, who was well known for his large onions and glorious blooms, always played a big part in the arrangements. As did Bill Smith and his son, John, from Hill Top nurseries, Thornton. Len Walker, of Bagworth, always grew a large marrow, and while it was still small and tender he would scratch on the skin, 'Cross Hills 1950', or some other relevant message. As the marrow grew, so did the message in equal proportions, the words standing out in an effective display as they calloused over.

Even in the house of God the unexpected can happen and it did, as the following amusing true incident illustrates. Sometime during the 1920's, when a 'perfect' Harvest Festival service was in progress, the solemnity of the occasion was temporarily shattered when one of God's little creatures decided to inspect the unexpected windfall of delicious food.

It was the custom at Harvest Festival time to stack up apples and other fruit in a tight pyramid on the ledge at the back of the pulpit, high at schoolroom level. This particular year Mr. Garnham was deep into preaching his sermon when a mouse decided to run to and fro across the ledge, in out of the fruit.

Of course, the inevitable happened; one of the apples was disturbed by the mouse and the whole lot came cascading down on Mr. Garnham, much to the amusement of the congregation.

The mellow aroma of harvest produce on entering the church was quite delightful. On the following Monday evening the sale of goods always took place in the Sunday school room. The current minister would be the 'auctioneer', which gave him license to air a favourite saying. Rev Garnham, for instance, would hold up a good solid cabbage, rap it with his knuckles and cry, 'This one has a heart as hard as the Parson's!'

Not all the garden produce was sold, as the offerings were prolific. Children would fill small baskets in attractive arrangements, as they still do, and they are taken afterwards to organisations, such as the Cheshire Homes. In recent years all the produce has been taken to Staunton Harold, a home for incurables near Ashby-de-la-Zouch.

During the war when food was scarce, most things made a good price and bidding was fierce. They were times of uncertainty and anguish, when we thought and prayed for our loved ones away on duty. But conversely, they were also times of wonderful fellowship on these special occasions within the church.

A typical Cross Hills Harvest Festival display.

CHRISTMAS AT CROSS HILLS

Cross Hills version of Christmas always started early— usually in late November with a Christmas Fayre. All down the ages the festive season was a time to celebrate and 'cash in' on this unique part of the season. On reading the minutes of meetings since 1900, the church has always looked to work hard towards this event. Garden parties, jumble sales, and sales of work have always been held throughout the year, but Christmas time was always 'special'.

Up until now, little has been said about the ladies of the church, mainly because they never held office. But as the old saying goes, 'Behind a good man is always a good woman', and this held true at Cross Hills.

The ladies always worked very hard throughout, particularly at bazaars, social occasions, spring and Christmas Fayres. They would cook and bake, demonstrate their sewing skills, fill pickle and preserving jars with mouth-watering fruit and veg. And they all sold like wildfire, boosting church funds. Needless to say, without this 'behind the scene' work, these events would never have succeeded.

One of the 'highlights' of Cross Hills Christmas was the carol singing on Christmas Eve. In the 1930's and during the second world war, singing was done in both Bagworth and Thornton. The singing started at 7pm and continued until 2am or 3am the next morning. This punishing schedule however, proved too much, so the two villages took it in turns to be entertained, making it a bi-annual occasion.

Bagworth was always the hardest work. Carol singers would start at Desford colliery, up Heath Road, along Main Street and Barlestone Road and then down the long, long stretch of Station Road, finishing at the 'Maynard Arms'. You might well have been ready for a pint or two but you'd be unlucky, because by then the pubs had been closed for hours!

An easier option was Thornton. The first stop after assembling at the chapel was Mr Shepherd's home, Park Farm— or Bagworth Moats, as it is identified on early maps. As observed by Mr Peter Willett, who was one of the carol singers, 'We were always made very welcome here and received a good donation to start us off.' After the 'Hollow' and 'Stag and Castle', we would walk up the hill and into Thornton's Main Street.

In those days there were no housing estates and fewer stops were required, so we sang our way straight down to Bill Smith's at 'Hill Top'.

When we had finished singing outside, Bill would say, 'Right, go into the house.' Inside, the table was laid out with all sorts of food. Ham sandwiches— there was always a salted pig hanging on the wall— salmon, cheese and pickle. And invariably, Alice had been baking mince pies and tarts, all to be washed down with copious cups of tea and coffee.

After a good chat and sing song, it was time to go home, only to find that John, (Bill and Alice's son), had locked the door and hidden the key!'

A Sunday School Hymn book used at Cross Hills in the 1970's. Compiled by Margaret V. Old and Elspeth M. Stephenson.

PART VI: OFFICERS OF THE CHURCH

CHAPTER 21

SUNDAY SCHOOL SUPERINTENDENTS

Tom Orme

Nothing is known about Superintendents at Cross Hills in the very early days. But on opening the time capsule found in the old church during demolition in 1995, much is written about the men, women and young ladies who were the teachers in 1885.

In the early 1900's Mr. Tom Orme was the Superintendent, and it appears that he was quite a character. He lived in the cottage at the bottom of School Lane in Bagworth.

As a hobby he kept bees and sold honey. In his front room he had a loom on which he made stockings for a living. There were many Orme's about in that day, so the people who were associated with him called him 'Stockiner Tom'! (from stockinger— a person who knits on a stocking frame).

Mr Tom Orme, Superintendent at Cross Hills.

A certain tale that has often been told amongst chapel circles relates to one Sunday morning when, with the Sunday school full of children, a certain mischief maker called Joe Twigger pulled out of his pocket a live sparrow. He released it to fly around the packed Sunday school, exclaiming loudly in perfect Bagworth/Thornton dialogue, 'There guz a bod!'

Of course, the children were in uproar, shouting and laughing. Tom, trying vainly to keep control, boomed, 'Come out here, Twigger— I'll tweak your ears!' Or, at least, that is what Tom **thought** he had said. But Tom could not pronounce his T's, so unfortunately his outburst caused even more uproar among the children when it came out as, '... Quigger— I'll Queak your ears!'

Tom Orme was Superintendent in the Sunday school for 50 years. On Tom's death, Mr. R. Blower of Ellistown was engaged, in 1931, not only to make a plaque in his honour, but also to unveil it, which he did one Sunday afternoon at a special service.

'...we have Special Services for that day and we ask Rev. E.J. Garnham to preach, and the choir to sing an Anthem at night.'

Memorial stone to Thomas Orme, 1847 - 1930

The Plaque is currently mounted in the new church porch, and reads:

Erected in Memory of
Thomas Orme
Superintendent of the Sunday
School for 50 Yrs & for many yrs.
A Deacon of the Church
Died Feb. 12th 1930
Aged 83 Yrs.

Thomas Walmsley

Some unforgettable characters became Sunday school Superintendents. One was Mr. Thomas Walmsley, who kept a sweet shop in Bagworth. He was popular with local children because he generously distributed sweets among them.

REAL-LIFE STORY No 5

William (Bill) Smith

Mr. William (Bill) Smith of Hill Top Nurseries, Thornton, took over the Sunday school during the 1939 - 1945 war.

Bill had a bad accident underground when he worked at Bagworth colliery, breaking his neck. He was taken to the Leicester Royal Infirmary and was paralysed from the neck downwards. To try to relieve the pressure on his spinal chord he had to have an operation to be put on 'traction' This led to a remarkable and unusual story which was thought to be worth relating.

Unfortunately for Bill when he was anaesthetised, unbeknown to the doctors and surgeons, he could still hear and sense what was going on, although he could not feel pain.

When he 'came round' and the nurses and surgeon visited him later on the ward, they were absolutely horrified when he repeated what they had said and done during the operation. Bill related how they had fitted a caliper to his head, and how a hole had to be bored into the bone on each side.

The nurse using the brace and bit said, 'His skull is really hard, can I use an electric drill?'

The surgeon replied, 'Of course not. Don't be so silly!'

Bill told them of the awful 'squeaking and grinding noises' and that he was glad when his ordeal was all over.

He was visited by the Rev. E. J. Garnham, who sympathised with Bill and told him, 'Never mind, laddie, underneath are the everlasting arms.'

Bill replied, 'Well, if they are, Lord, let me feel them.' And in Bill's own words, immediately, like a 'whip lash' the feeling was restored to his body!

After his miraculous cure of paralysis, Bill was to spend many more years in the Sunday school organising the displays that were put on by the children, and doing much good work.

Bill Smith had several hobbies, one of which was competing at horticultural shows. He is shown here exhibiting some of his favourite chrysanthemums.

On April 23rd 1947 Mr. William Smith suggested that to interest young people from the Sunday school, they should be invited to join the active choir. When this suggestion was taken up, several Sunday school members became talented choristers who thrived on their new-found singing skills.

Mr. William Smith, Sunday school Superintendent, organised a demonstration by the scholars on

Mr William (Bill) Smith of Hill Top Nurseries, Superintendent 1939 - 1945

December 7th 1947. This included the children bringing gifts of toys during the service to be sent to the Mission Station at Jamtara, India, where Mr. Ken Smith was a Missionary. The day's collections were also given to this cause.

Mr Clifford farmer, Deacon, Choirmaster & Superintendent from late 40's - 1968. Cliff loved a sing-song round the piano.

Clifford Farmer

The next Superintendent was Mr. Clifford Farmer, who had been brought up in the Sunday school from a lad. He was a very good pianist and had learned to play the organ under Mr. Elijah Baxter of Ellistown. Cliff worked in the Sunday school from the late 1940's, staying until he moved to Leicester in 1968.

Of course, music played an extremely prominent part in the Sunday school and were considered by many as being very fortunate having such a versatile and talented person as Cliff as their Choirmaster, Organist and Superintendent.

Sheila Whitmore

Miss Sheila Whitmore was recommended by the Sunday school teachers for the post of Sunday school Superintendent. This was passed unanimously on February 28th 1967 on behalf of the Church.

Sheila worked very hard for Cross Hills Sunday school, organising such events as demonstrations, at a time when there were many scholars attending. Children often participated in 'Special Services' within the church, and the Sunday school was very well organised.

Mrs. Sheila Langton (nee Whitmore) remained Sunday school Superintendent until 1977.

Miss Sheila Whitmore – a very good Superintendent from 1967 - 1977.

CHAPTER 22

SECRETARIES

We have looked at Choirmasters and Sunday school Superintendents, now let us look at the Secretaries. These officers, together with Treasurers, are the 'back room boys' who do great work with, quite often, little to show for it.

Mr Chas. Massey of 'Reservoir Farm' Thornton. The first recorded Secretary after 1900.

Charles Massey

The first Secretary recorded in the minutes after 1900 (no minutes can be found prior) was Mr. Charles Massey of Reservoir Farm, Thornton. The position of Chairman of the meetings was usually taken by the Minister, and the Secretary sat at the side writing down the minutes.

Meetings were long and much business was discussed, with as many as 20 items on the agenda. When the Secretary finally wrote, '...and the meeting closed in prayer', it must indeed have been a relief.

Mr Abraham Willett, Secretary 1905 - 1909. He caught pneumonia and died aged 40.

Abraham Willett

The next Secretary was Mr. Abraham Willett. He was a miner from Coleorton. In 1903 one of the Bagworth Colliery shafts needed shortening, widening and straightening, a complex operation. Abraham landed the job as undermanager and supervised the project.

He was Secretary of Coleorton Baptist Chapel, and his family were all members there. When he left, to bring his family of seven to live at Bagworth in 1905, he was presented with an inscribed silver coffee pot for his work at Coleorton.

All his family attended Cross Hills and it was not long after he settled down at Bagworth that he was made Secretary of Cross Hills. Unfortunately, in 1909 he caught pneumonia and died on February 6th aged only 40 years.

W. E. Bland

Mr. W. E. Bland took over the vacant office of Secretary on Sunday January 3rd 1909 and did 15 years good service. (See photograph under music section)

John Farmer

Mr John Farmer, who also came to Bagworth to work at the colliery, became a Secretary at Cross Hills. He hailed from Harpole, in Northamptonshire, and came to this area about 1904.

Mr John Farmer, Secretary 1924 - 1951

An entry recorded in the first minute book about John Farmer was on March 21st 1905. He was on a list of church members to help with the public tea and entertainment to celebrate the refurbishment of the church. While the church was closed for a few weeks, services had been held in Mr. Hill's barn!

Mr. Farmer took over the Office of Secretary on April 8th 1924 from Mr. Bland. John became a long and faithful servant to Cross Hills, holding the position of Secretary for 27 years. John died on November 24th, 1954, agcd 76 years.

Mr Ernest Harris

There have been very few changes of secretaries at Cross Hills since 1900, mainly due to the fact that most have covered many years in office. Mr. Ernest Harris, who was born in Bagworth and attended Cross Hills Sunday school as a boy, joined the church and subsequently became Assistant Secretary in 1947 and full Secretary in 1951. Ernie did a marathon 'stint' before retiring in 1994.

At a meeting held on March 28th 1951 Mr Harris assumed the full responsibility of Secretary. Mr. Harris's dedicated work for Cross Hills, especially in the 1980's when negotiations with the National Coal Board over subsidence damage to the 1885 chapel were in progress, was a particularly frustrating and difficult time for him.

With hindsight, if this work had not been done with the thoroughness and determination shown by Mr Harris, the new 1996 chapel may never have been built at all.

His total spell as Assistant Secretary and Secretary totalled 47 years of faithful service. All good things have to come to an end, and so it was that Mr. Ernest Harris finally retired from the post of Secretary on March 30th 1994.

Mr Ernest Harris, Secretary of Cross Hills from 1947 - 1994, 47 years of faithful service, shown with Mrs Harris at the Centenary Celebrations.

Robert Holmes

Mr. Robert Holmes expressed his willingness to take up this important and challenging office, and was unanimously voted in as Cross Hills new Secretary on the evening of March 30th 1994. Robert took over this responsible position at the age of 19, and must have been the youngest Secretary of Cross Hills ever.

Mr Robert Holmes.

CHAPTER 23

TREASURERS

Throughout the whole life of Cross Hills, according to the minutes of the meetings, the church has always been short of money, down the ages, and the Treasurer's lot 'was not a happy one!' (With apologies to Gilbert and Sullivan!) Several times, money was lent to the church by deacons and members, to be paid back if and when sufficient funds could eventually be raised.

Money was raised by Samuel Deacon, who kept subscription lists in notebooks. But it was obvious from reading his remarks in these account books, that collecting due monies from patrons was not always easy. Comments by Deacon and his successors were written against the names of members in arrears with their subs, like *'nothing'* and *'could give!'*

(See BAPTIST CHAPEL – in 'NO-MAN'S LAND' Chapter 5)

Jim Hill: First 'Recorded' Treasurer

The Treasurer at Cross Hills in 1900 was Jim Hill of Manor Farm, Bagworth, who resigned in 1906.

William Prime

Mr William Prime proved to be a real stalwart by taking over in 1908 and serving faithfully as Treasurer for 42 years, before submitting to retirement in 1950 at the age of 82!

William once said that he never realised he was getting old until he was turned 80.

(Photo in 'Music' section.)

Tom Prime

In 1950 William handed the account books over into the capable hands of Tom, his son, who managed to keep the Treasurer's position in the family for a further 28 years. Tom retired from office on February 14th 1978 at the age of 73.

Mr Tom Prime, Treasurer at Cross Hills for 28 years 1950 - 1978.

Peter Willett

Tom's nephew, Peter Willett, took charge of Cross Hills books in 1978, and is still the Treasurer to date. This means that during almost the whole of the 20th century only three people— all from the same family— have held the post of Treasurer.

Mr Peter Willett, Deacon, Carried on the family tradition as Treasurer from 1978 to the present day.

CHAPTER 24

LAY PREACHERS

90 year old Mr L.T. Childs, Lay Preacher. He officiated at Cross Hills from the early 1940's.

L. T. Childs

In order to 'fill the pulpit' when the Minister and Pastor were otherwise engaged, the church has always made use of lay preachers. They were employed regularly, particularly when one minister had three or more churches to look after and his work needed to be shared. Most lay preachers, especially in the old days, were local men who volunteered to do the work with no financial reward. Some were able to travel over greater distances as transport and roads began to improve.

Cross Hills has always benefited from larger churches, such as Melbourne Hall in Leicester, who have sent out their members to help out the smaller churches in this way. Some 'local preachers' have spent the bulk of their working lives in this manner.

A fine example of longevity of one visiting preacher is Mr L.T. Childs, who preached at Cross Hills in the early 1940's and returned recently to conduct Mrs Garnham's funeral service in November 1996— incidentally, the first funeral to be held since the 1996 church was operational.

Cross Hills will always be indebted to these unselfish men and women who have dedicated themselves to the work of the Lord, and nearly always in their 'leisure time'.

This Hymn book was used at Cross Hills by the Young People's Fellowship during and after Billy Graham's Evangelical Campaign to the U.K.

CHAPTER 25

CENTENARY CELEBRATIONS

At the Church meeting of May 4th 1984 important arrangements were forging ahead for the Centenary Celebrations of August 3rd 1985. One of the most important attractions was a brass band, and the band for the big day was that of Hinckley Salvation Army.

Arrangements were made for a public tea, with a film show in the evening. A suggestion was made to stage an exhibition of old photographs, Bibles, registers and programmes of events from 100 years ago. **Programme for the day: Parade, 3.00pm; public Tea, 4.30pm; Evening Session, including film show, to commence at 6.00pm.**

1885-1985

CROSS HILLS

BAPTIST CHURCH

PART OF THE BARTON GROUP

Situated between Bagworth & Thornton

CENTENARY CELEBRATIONS

AUGUST 3rd – 18th 1985

SATURDAY AUGUST 17th

CELEBRATION RALLY & MINISTERS ANNIVERSARY

Commencing 7.00 pm

GUEST SPEAKER

Rev. Bernard Green M.A.B.D., General Secretary of the Baptist Union.

SUNDAY AUGUST 18th

UNITED SERVICES OF THE BARTON GROUP

10.30 am and 6.00 pm.

PREACHER

Rev. Bernard Green, M.A.B.D.

We are serving lunches after the morning service, why not come and join us. Please try to let us know if you are interested before August 1st (phone Mary Holmes on Bagworth 624) so that correct numbers can be catered for. A nominal charge of £1.50 adults, 50p children will be made to cover costs.

Deacons and members at the Cross Hills Centenary celebrations 1985.

PART VII: MINING SUBSIDENCE

CHAPTER 26

THE FIGHT FOR COMPENSATION BEGINS: SPECIAL MINING REPORT

Subsidence Special

When Samuel Deacon junior, Jacob Brewin and their followers chose the site for the first chapel at Cross Hills in 1813, away from Lord Maynard's ground, little did they realise that they had chosen a site which would later prove to be a great deal of trouble. Ironically, if the planners could have purchased land a few hundred yards away and up the hill from the 'Stag and Castle' towards Thornton, the church would never have suffered from mining subsidence damage.

However, this first chapel was built 10 years before the Bagworth colliery shafts were sunk in 1823, and approximately on the line of the eastern boundary of the Leicestershire coalfield. The boundary is formed by a massive landslip called, 'The Thringstone Fault'. This fault runs roughly in a north-west – south-east direction and through 'The Hollow' near to Cross Hills.

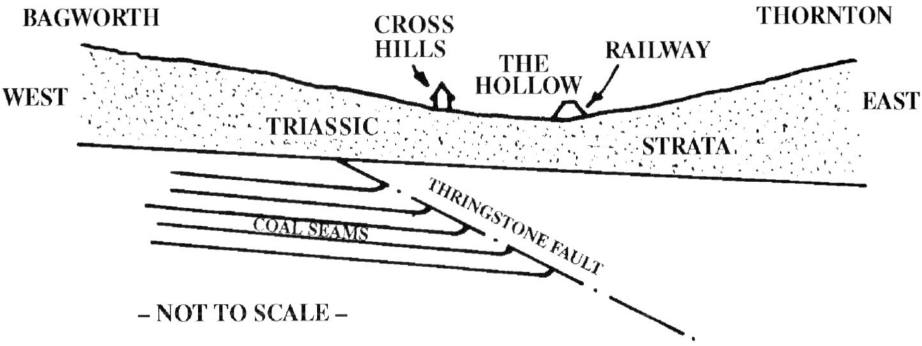

Sketch showing section East - West between Bagwoth and Thornton, through Cross Hills Chapel and 'The Hollow'.

Three collieries have worked up to, or very near to this fault from the west: Ellistown, Bagworth and Desford, and all damaged Cross Hills with their workings at one time or another. Altogether, 17 feet of coal was extracted from directly underneath the chapel, causing untold damage to the property. As was also the case in Barlestone Road, Heath Road and the Parish Church of Holy Rood. All the properties on these roads had to be completely demolished, Bagworth village having been decimated.

The first mining subsidence damage was recorded at Cross Hills as early as 1931. Subsequent deterioration became progressively worse and accelerated through the years as more coal seams were worked directly below. The final coal to be 'won' was regarded as the 'cream' of all the seams, being extremely high in quality and the deepest. This was the 7 feet 6 inches thick Lower Main Seam, and was extracted from under the chapel in 1978 by Desford colliery.

Ground movement from subsidence takes a long time to finally settle down, so although 18 years had elapsed since the last coal seam had been extracted, special measures had to be taken to strengthen the foundations of the new 1996 church. This took the form of large quantities of steel reinforcement set into the compacted concrete.

CHAPTER 27

FIRST INSTANCE OF MINING SUBSIDENCE. BUILDING A NEW, SAFE CHURCH?

Subsidence: First Recorded Instance.

June 10th 1931 saw the first recorded instance of coal mining subsidence damage to the church. Mr. R. Blower was asked if he would approach the Ellistown Colliery Company and ask them whether they would be prepared to 'help us in the repairing of walls caused by getting coals nearby.'

Cracks Appear in the Buildings

At the meeting of September 18th 1946 there was a concerned discussion about the various cracks appearing in the walls of the Sunday school room. Concern about land subsidence took on a new urgency, when on March 10th 1948 it was noticed that the wall had become subject to movement at the front of the church building.

The National Coal Board was approached as far back as March 10th 1948 and again on September 8th 1954 regarding subsidence damage to floors and doors.

Going Down Like the Titanic? Time for action!
Vision of a New Safe Church— or is it Just a Mirage?

For the first time since October 1986, when letters were sent out to the membership asking what was to be done with the old building, serious seeds of thought again started to flourish about the possibility of building a brand new church. The old building had served well, but subsidence had now riddled the 1885 church structure so badly that, like the Titanic, it would surely 'go under'. If nothing drastic was done to alter the situation very soon, the building would disintegrate before their eyes. But members of Cross Hills were not to be disheartened: they had vision and tenacity— and they were going to win through with the guidance of the Lord.

A Loughborough builder, Mr. Dennis Mott, was contacted and invited to visit members of the Church. It was already known that he had erected a very pleasing House of God somewhere in Loughborough.

The Church Building Committee assembled on the evening of June 14th 1990 at the church with the builder. They took him on a tour of all the property, inside and out, in order to get his expert opinion. Armed with the builder's recommendation, the Committee concluded that it would be more economical to construct a smaller, purpose built church than to repair the old.

The Loughborough builder discussed the various options open.

1) Repair the old building — the cost of which would have been prohibitive.
2) Erect prefabricated buildings constructed in units.
3) Or build in brick and slate, a place 30 feet by 30 feet, designed in such a way that would allow for future expansion.

At this time, the builder was looking to construct on the car park, where it was possible, with permission, to erect a building. During the meeting of October 20th 1990 the decision was taken to instruct the builder to submit Outline Planning to the District Council.

Keeping all Options Open

To keep all options open, a small committee met a Representative from Hinckley & Bosworth Borough Council to hear advice on the situation of the old church buildings. These, we heard, were repairable but would need some underpinning of walls at the foundations. Also, stronger tie bars were required to prevent further spreading of the walls.

There also was a problem with water collecting under the building. To control this it would be necessary for a deep drainage system to be installed. The aim was to divert water from the hillside enabling it to flow around the church and so keep clear of the foundations. Unfortunately, it was felt that these alterations would incur prohibitive costs.

The Battle With British Coal Looms

December 12 1966: the National Coal Board made a grant of £225 to Cross Hills towards the Church's decoration.

February 20th 1973: a surveyor from Ripley agreed to look after the interests of the Church regarding subsidence and made a survey.

March 22nd 1983: the NCB said that they were not responsible for the leaking roof.

October 27th 1986: special meeting to discuss the greatly damaged building. Letters were sent out to 17 members asking what was preferred. 16 out of 17 wanted a new church, rather than have the old one repaired.

Mr Barfield, Secretary of the Baptist Union Trustees, was informed that the NCB (who had now changed their name to British Coal) had refused to carry out repairs and had offered only very low compensation. Litigation and legal action was next agreed upon.

Mark Webb-Sear, the BU solicitor, prepared the necessary documents, and a barrister was employed to defend the case for the Church.

The surveyor employed by Cross Hills was unable to obtain a better deal from British Coal, which amounted to only £45,055 plus £4,500 for a temporary building. At this time, the surveyor had advised Cross Hills not to accept this offer.

A barrister, engaged by the Church, produced a booklet entitled: 'Opinion' in which he outlined BC's procedure for Limitation and what was required to prepare a case for Litigation. This, in effect, informed Cross Hills that they 'did not have enough evidence' against BC. To gain sufficient evidence there should have been, during the previous six years, photographs taken, 'tell-tale' recorders fixed across cracks and pledges from officers, both written and recorded.

On October 2nd 1989 the Church was advised by the Surveyor to accept the sum of £49,555 compensation (including payment for a temporary building) from British Coal. They did this, as it was 'Hobson's Choice', but were very disappointed that this compensation awarded was minimal compared with the damage that B.C. had done. This was the story of 'David and Goliath' in reverse! In this case, David was on the receiving end! So, reluctantly, Cross Hills had to accept British Coal's original offer, the former having the opinion that they had been badly let down by the surveyor whom the Church had employed.

Searching Every Avenue

Another idea, with no guarantee, was to negotiate with British Coal to determine if they would be willing to exchange sufficient ground within the village of Bagworth to build a new church. This would be in exchange for the present church buildings. If this project went ahead, members felt it was imperative to ensure the new church was built on stable ground free from future subsidence.

Cross Hills also tried to negotiate with BC to exchange the Church, but excluding the graveyard, for the old Bagworth colliery offices, and convert them into a church. However, British Coal were not interested in that idea.

A feasibility study was carried out to see what could be done.

Feasibility Study Offered

The main business at the meeting of June 6th 1990 was to hear the report of the Civil Engineers, with regard to the estimated cost of making the church safe. A rough estimate showed the cost would be over £54,000 which was far more money than the Church could afford merely to make it safe and secure.

With the approval of the Rural Development Commission, a feasibility study was offered to test the viability of repairing the property. The study would cost an estimated £5,000, of which the R.D.C. would pay half. The other half would be split equally between Hinckley & Bosworth Borough Council and the Baptist Union Corporation Ltd. In real terms Cross Hills would be responsible for paying £1,250 which was agreed.

Prepared by Pick Everard, Architects, Surveyors and Consulting Engineers, the study was designed to:

1) Establish the current condition of the building fabric,
2) Identify and cost any building repairs required and
3) Assess any work required to alter the buildings for other uses.

The conclusion came as no surprise when the study confirmed that the church was in a very bad condition. Buildings needed new mechanical and electrical installations, besides the serious repairs already apparent, to achieve an acceptable standard of accommodation.

In terms of future use, the best of several options put forward appeared to favour partial demolition, namely of the Sunday school rooms. The body of the main chapel could be repaired, they said, and a new building then added, attaching it to the rear of the old chapel.

As for the costing, repairs to the chapel alone, without the new building, amounted to £125,000. But taking into account VAT, Statutory Authority Fees, professional fees, and so on, repairing the old church was not a viable proposition and was totally out of the question.

Plans discussed

Plans that were drawn up by Pick Everard of a new church were not thought practical for Cross Hills. Two drawings by Mr. Peter Willett were discussed and deemed to be much nearer to the design envisaged. The drawings were inspected and passed by 9 out of 13 people at a church meeting held on September 8th, 1993. Consequently, Pick Everard were instructed to produce plans on the lines submitted in Peter's drawings. This they did, and the new plans were promptly submitted to Hinckley & Bosworth Borough Council's Planning Department to 'test the water'.

Meanwhile, a new Lay Pastor is engaged.

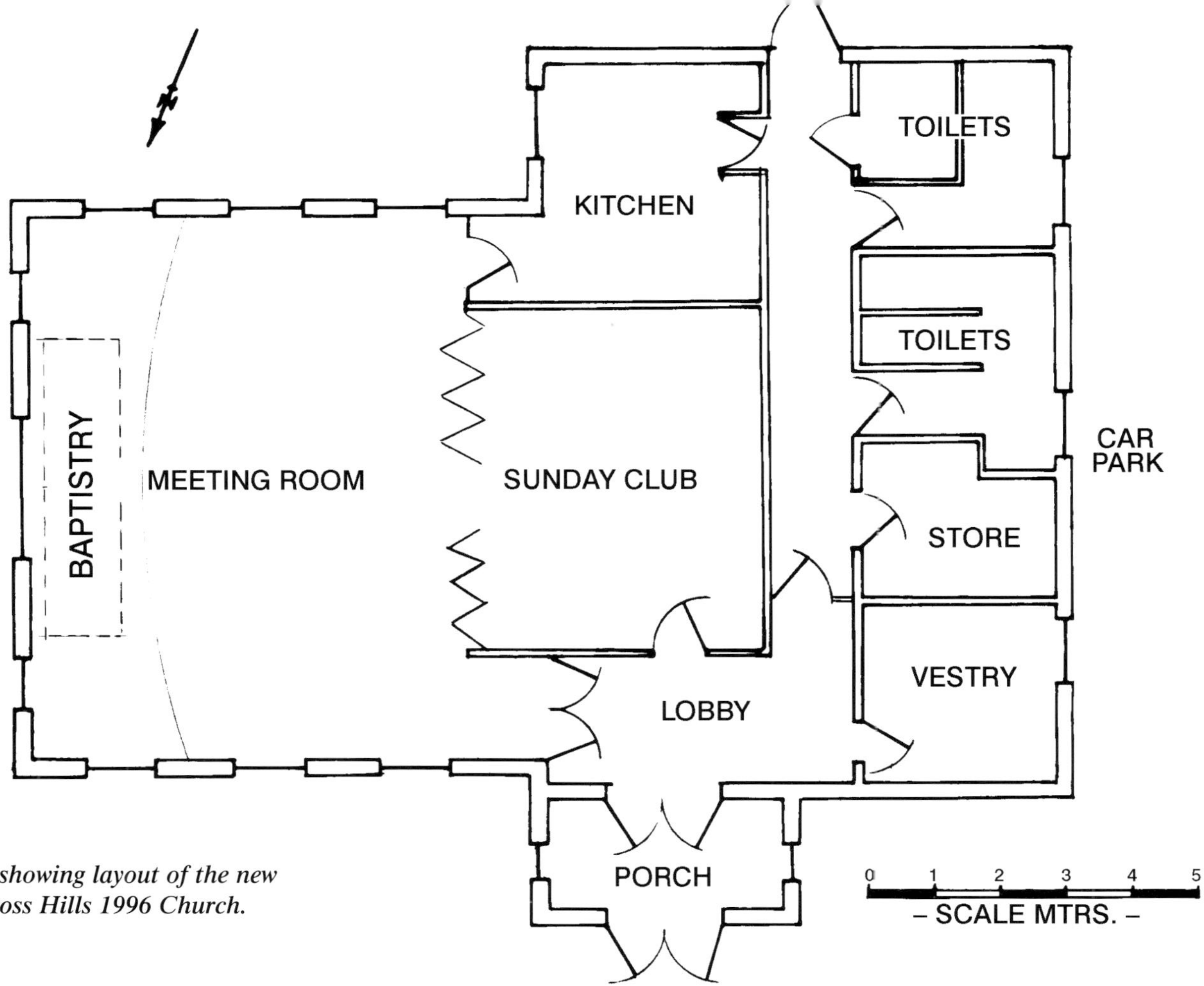

Plan showing layout of the new Cross Hills 1996 Church.

CHAPTER 28

LAY PASTOR IS ENGAGED

Full Time Minister to Cease

At the Deacons' General Church Meeting it was concluded that, due to their financial position, it was no longer possible to engage the services of a full-time Minister. However, it did seem a viable proposition to engage a Lay Pastor for each church in the group—namely Barton, Barlestone and Cross Hills— whose expenses would be met from the General Church funds.

Pastor, Garry Kelly and his wife, Lynda: their drive and enthusiasm soon had things moving.

Mr. Garry Kelly, of Barwell, was invited to become Lay Pastor of Cross Hills Church on June 17th 1991. He expressed his wish to accept the invitation regardless of payment. He and his wife, Lynda transferred their membership from Earl Shilton Baptist Church to Cross Hills.

The engagement was taken a step further on November 4th when Garry was formally accepted by a unanimous show of hands and it was recorded that he was now the official Pastor. On Saturday September 21st the Induction Service was held before a large congregation.

The Petal Window

A further section of the Petal Window was reported to be damaged on November 11th 1991, allowing much cold and dampness into the building. The heating of the subsidence riddled church was now causing serious problems. Mr Garry Kelly, Cross Hills Pastor, approached Mr. Roger Hemsley, of Alan Underwood Ltd., builders, to obtain estimates and advice.

It must be stressed that a great deal of sentiment was, and is still, attached to the beautiful petal window incorporated into the church building. It was, therefore, with much sadness that it was reported, on February 24th 1992, that this petal window, situated at the front of the old church, was now in a very dilapidated state, so the renewal of panes of glass was carried out immediately as a matter of urgency.

Old Iron Cross

One of the features of the 1885 chapel was the old iron cross, mounted on the roof. The old rugged cross caught the attention of visitors the moment the church came into view. It was mounted on a hefty sandstone block high on the gable end of the roof, nearest the road.

Sometime during the 1980's the whole hefty cross assembly was dislodged, perhaps by adverse weather, a strong wind— or a more feasible answer was probably subsidence from mining. Anyway, it became unseated and fell to the right-hand side, into the car park. It was stored in the graveyard, but later mysteriously disappeared. This was disappointing as the intention was to incorporate the old iron cross as a feature in the memorial garden of the new church.

The old 'rugged' Cross: caught the attention of visitors.

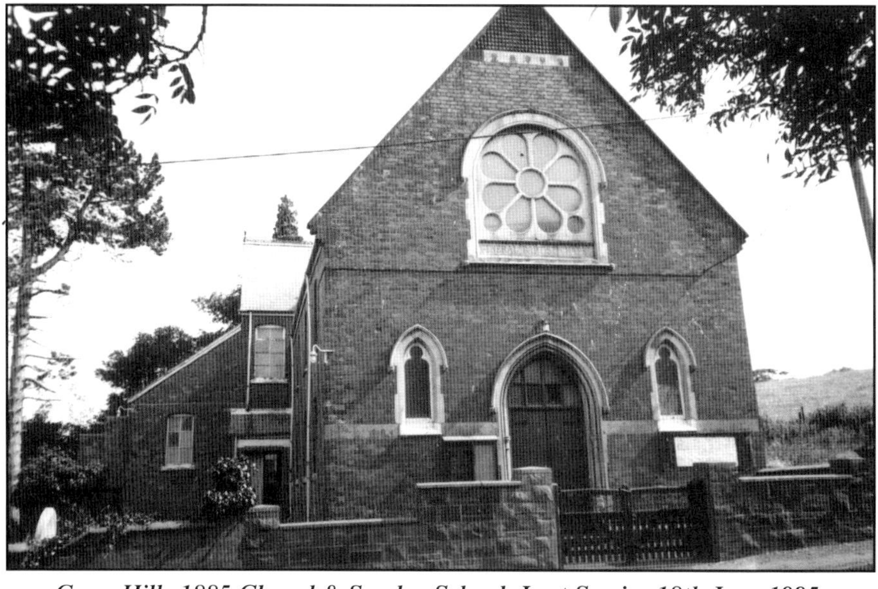

Cross Hills 1885 Chapel & Sunday School: Last Service 18th June 1995.

PART VIII: VISIONS OF A NEW CHURCH

CHAPTER 29

THE PLANNING STAGE

Building Fund Opened

A new Building Fund account was opened from January 28th 1991. Meanwhile, news from the District Council regarding our Outline Planning application was now available. They stated that no less than Full Planning Permission would be necessary before it could even be considered. All members of the Church were very disappointed with this decision, as this would incur high costs for Architect's plans to be drawn up, with no guarantee at the end of the day that they would be accepted.

Building Committee is Formed: Plans are Passed

It was learned on April 20th, 1994, that the church building plans had been passed by Hinckley & Bosworth Borough Council, with a few conditions attached. These included regrading the car park and modifying the entrance and exit to prevent sludge and hardcore falling on the road.

How the Money Grew

By February 24th 1992, with accumulated interest, the total funds held by East Midland Baptist Association on behalf of Cross Hills' now stood at £58,412. Further investment with the E.M.B.A. up until March 24th 1993, saw the Building Fund climb to £63,000.

A Ring of Change: New Architect Introduced

A new Architect by the name of Mr. Ken Payne, of Kirkby Mallory, was introduced to the Church by Garry Kelly on July 4th 1994. Mr. Payne explained to members his work and expenses charged for drawing up detailed plans right up to tendering stage. For an extra fee he was willing to supervise the building of the church.

This point marked a radical change in the thinking and planning of the new church. Up until this time the new building was going to be attached to the old church at the rear. Ken Payne gave the opinion that we could demolish the old chapel completely at this juncture and simply build the new one on the cleared plot. It was pointed out by Garry Kelly that in spite of the thousands of pounds already spent on the project, not one brick had yet been laid.

CHAPTER 30

SALVAGING STRATEGY PLANNED

Salvaging Key Parts

If the old church was to be pulled down, it was suggested that certain key parts of the structure could be salvaged and incorporated into the new place of worship. Such prime objects like the petal window could be carefully preserved. The meeting ended leaving members with plenty to think about.

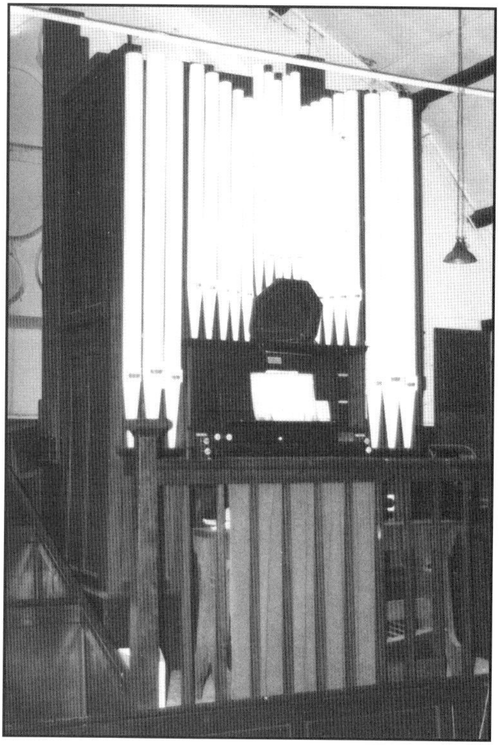

Sad goodbye to the beloved Bedwell Pipe Organ.

Sad Goodbye's to the Beloved Bedwell Pipe Organ

Storage of furniture from the old church while the building programme was in progress was quite a problem, and as Mr. Payne pointed out, storage was a very expensive item.

Mr. Ernie Harris queried whether it was possible for the organ in the old church to be resited in the new. Upon measuring, it was found that there would be insufficient height and space in the new building.

However much the desire, it would not be a viable proposition. Cross Hills' Bedwell 2-manuel pipe organ needed to be dismantled, repaired, retuned and reassembled, a job for the highly specialised, and all the expense that went with it. The approximate cost of reconditioning was expected to be around £10,000 which the church could not afford.

Finally, after much soul-searching, Mr. Peter Collins, an organ builder from Melton Mowbray bought the organ. He restored it completely and sold it to Mavesyn Ridware Parish Church, in Staffordshire, where it now stands in all its glory. It was, perhaps, some consolation to Cross Hills members that the organ had 'gone to a good home'

Demolition Agreed

Rev. Peter Grange, the Area Superintendent, chaired the meeting of July 25th 1994. All agreed to Ken Payne's amended and detailed drawings and to move forward with the demolition of the old chapel and the building of the new. A Building Committee was formed on November 13th 1994 consisting of Chairman, Peter Willett; Colin Harris; Mary Holmes; Ernie Harris; Garry Kelly; and Robert Holmes.

Because certain parts of the old church were to be auctioned off to raise money, such as old timber galleries, pulpit and pews, it was pointed out by Mr. Payne that the old buildings would have to be dismantled brick by brick rather than demolished, to avoid wrecking the good stuff.

The 'Bedwell' Organ now fully restored in Mavesyn Ridware Parish Church, Staffs.

That Joyful Feeling: Plans really take off!

Getting Down to Work

On Wednesday December 7th 1994 a site meeting was held to inform a representative of the church of the latest developments. There was much to discuss and suddenly, after years of wrangling and our failure to secure from British Coal what we believed to be our rights, there was now a wonderful, joyful feeling that our vision of building a new House of God would finally reach fruition.

Things were really taking off. Now that all the plans were laid out, the end product could be clearly seen. To help members who could not read the plans, Peter Willett made a scale model.

Items to be carefully dismantled for re-erection in the new building included, three main windows, three slate memorial plaques and two brass plaques. Some articles were deemed to be unsuitable in the new church, such as the organ, pews, pulpit and Baptistry. These were earmarked for sale to a firm specialising in such secondhand commodities. Things for storage included memorial tables and wooden chairs.

The District Council requested that Ken Payne should forward to them a plan, supplied by British Coal, showing the geological section under the church. The sectional plan needed to indicate to the Council what coal seams had been worked directly below the church and also where coal extraction had occurred under the surrounding vicinity. A supporting letter from British Coal was also sought by the Council.

Model of new 1996 Cross Hills Church made after the design stage by Mr Peter Willett to enable members to better understand the plans.

CHAPTER 31

Suitable Tender Accepted

Plans and specifications were sent out to six contractors throughout the County during January and February 1995. These covered the dismantling of the old church and the erection of the new one. The returned tenders were opened by Pastor Garry Kelly and Architect Ken Payne in the presence of the church Building Committee.

The lowest and successful tender of £110,654 was returned by R.J.H. Building Construction, of Thringstone, whose managing director was Mr. Roger Hemsley. By making certain shrewd savings on the specification of the new building, the adjusted tender was subsequently reduced to £102,709.

It was anticipated that with the cost of new furnishings and added overhead expenses, approximately £120,000 would be needed to complete the work. In real terms, only £80,000 was at the church's disposal at this time, leaving the need to raise another £40,000. This was considered to be an excessively large debt for the church to take on, so it was decided to undertake only the bare necessities for the time being. The aim was to make the church as habitable as possible until the money 'ran out', so to speak.

However, by members and friends working really hard at fund raising, mainly organised by Mr. Keith Holmes and family, and investing wisely in the East Midlands Baptist Association banking accounts, by the time the building was actually completed, only £12,000 was outstanding. This amount was borrowed from the Baptist Building Fund for the purpose of furnishing the new church.

CHAPTER 32

R.J.H. CONSTRUCTION STARTS DEMOLITION

Huge Salvage Operation Begins.

The Altar rail and balustrading was removed, together with a host of music, books and many other valuable items. The furniture was taken away and stored, some by a specialist firm, and the rest in some members' garages!

The demolition started on Friday July 7th 1995 and finished on August 17th of that year. It was done in such a way that several important features were saved and reincorporated into the new church. All the slate and brass memorial plaques were stored. So were the ridge tiles and finials, the two front windows and petal window surrounds. The stone limbs of the petal window were so completely decayed and crumbling that they had to be recreated in hardwood.

At the front of the chapel, the oak gates donated by Mrs. Roberts (past organist), were taken down, stored and refurbished before their re-erection in the graveyard patio area.

During the course of dismantling the 1885 chapel an exciting discovery was made. A time capsule was uncovered within the brickwork, near the front entrance.

Start of demolition 1995

Demolition well under way.

Demolition complete, with old foundations left intact for Memorial Garden enclosure.

The three old windows stored in a field.

Time capsule and assorted bricks from the 1885 chapel and stone from the 1814 chapel.

PART IX: BUILDING CROSS HILLS BAPTIST CHURCH – NUMBER THREE

CHAPTER 33

OPENING THE TIME CAPSULE

Victorian Glass Bottle

The time capsule held a fascinating slice of local history, when it was found in a cavity of the brickwork by the side of the main front doors. The Victorian glass bottle was not broken, which was a 'miracle' in its own right

The Past Uncovered

In late August 1995 Cross Hills members gathered at the home of Mr. Keith and Mrs. Mary Holmes with the specific assignment of opening the Time Capsule, which proved to contain much valuable information on what life was like over a century ago.

One of the most revealing items in the bottle was a letter written by the Sunday school Secretary, 20-year-old George Johnson. He explained that the capsule was concealed when the premises were built in 1885, replacing the original chapel which had stood on the site since 1814.

Opening the Time capsule at the home of Mr. Keith Holmes.

The Letter of George S. Johnson, Secretary of the Sunday School.

This bottle was deposited on Tuesday July 21st 1885 in the reign of Queen Victoria in the event of the laying of the six memorial stones laid by the following gentlemen.

1) Mr. R. Kirkman	*Cosby*
2) Mr Councillor George Payne	*Leicester*
3) Mr Councillor Joseph Wilford	*Leicester*
4) Mr H. Bott	*Leicester*
5) Mr Joseph Johnson	*Bagworth*
6) Mr John Orme	*Bagworth*

This chapel is a branch of the Barton Church with the Reverend George Needham, Barton, and the Reverend J. R. Godfrey, Barlestone, as pastors, and I. Deacon, Barton; J. Compton, Newton; E. Smith, Nailstone Wood; George Maides, Mkt. Bosworth; William Bridgett, Nailstone Wood; A. Swann, Desford; William Banton, Bagworth; J. Findley, Ibstock; R. C. Chawner, Desford, as Lay Preachers, and Messrs. I. Deacon, Barton; J. Compton, Newton; Thomas Wilkins, Barlestone; T. Smith, Thurcaston; J. Hayward, Twycross; C. Kirkman, Barton; T. Orme, Thornton; J. Price, Stapleton; J. Cart, Desford, are the Deacons for this foresaid Church.

The number of scholars at the present time is 125, with T. Orme and J. P. Henshaw as Superintendents, and George Orme, T. Marvin, J. Price, J. T. Lawrence, George S. Johnson, H. Orme, J. Hoxford, Miss S. B. Lawrence, E. Lawrence, Francis Holland, A. Smith, M. Johnson, E. Blower as teachers.

The name of the vicar of this Parish is the Rev. S. Adams. The Members of Parliament for this Division are J. J. Paget, Esq., Liberal, and A. Pell, Esq., Conservative.

The Presidents of the General Baptist Association is the Rev. W. Evans of Leicester.

John Wills, Esq. of Derby is the Architect, and Mr. William Needham of Loughborough, contractor for this building.

The new plot of land, which the school rooms are built on, was purchased and given by Mr. J. Johnson, Senior, Bagworth.

This was wrote by George S. Johnson, Secretary of this Sunday school, on July 20th, 1885, aged 20.

Reduced copy of George S. Johnson's letter. He was 20 years old and was secretary of Cross Hills Sunday school.

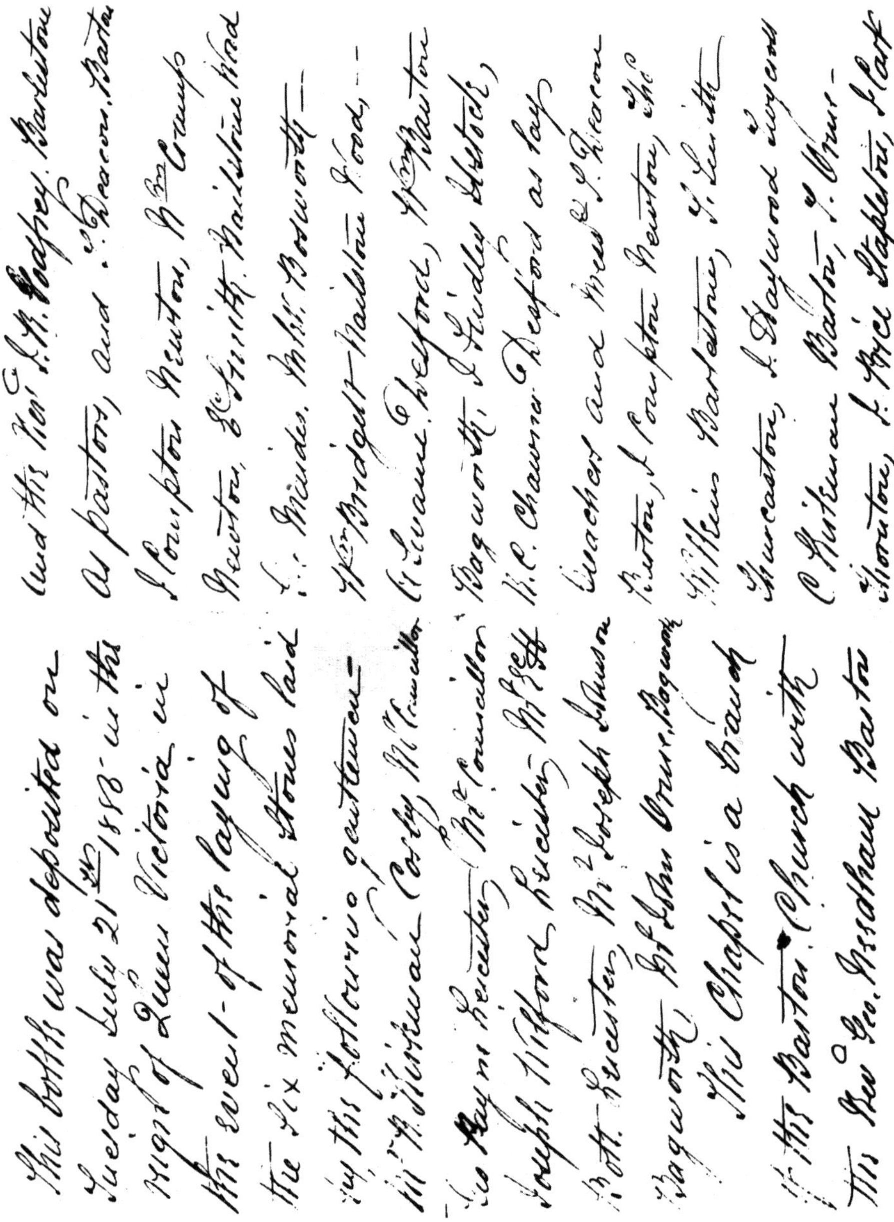

1

This bottle was deposited on
Tuesday July 21st 1885 in the
reign of Queen Victoria in
the event of the laying of
the six memorial stones laid
by the following gentlemen—
Mr R. Kirkman Cosby, Mr Councillor
Geo Payne Leicester, Mr Councillor
Joseph Wilford Leicester, Mr E H
Bott. Leicester, Mr Joseph Johnson
Bagworth, Mr John Orme, Bagworth

This Chapel is a branch
of the Barton Church with
the Revd Geo. Needham Barton

2

and the Revd J. R. Godfrey. Barlestone
as pastors, and J. Deacon. Barton
J Compton Newton, Wm Cramp
Newton, E Smith. Nailstone Wood
[illegible] Minders. Mkt Bosworth—
Wm Bridgett Nailstone Wood,—
A Swann Desford, Wm Barton
Bagworth, J Findley Ibstock,
R.C. Chawner Desford as lay
preachers and Messrs J. Deacon
Barton, J Compton Newton, Thos
Wilkins Barlestone, J. Smith
Thurcaston, J. Haywood Twycross
C Kirkman Barton, J. Orme—
Thornton, J. Price Stapleton, J Cart

The letter was dated July 20th 1885, was placed in the time capsule, which was then hidden in the brickwork of the church on Tuesday July 21st.

3

Welford are the 'Deacons' for
the foresaid Church.
The numbers of Scholars
at the present time is 125. with
[illegible] Orme, Senr and Geo Henshaw
as Superintendents and Geo Orme
[illegible] Munnis, J Prince, J T Lawrence
[illegible] J Johnson, H Orme, J. Hoxford
[illegible] Holland, Miss S. B. Lawrence
[illegible] Lawrence, E Orme. A. Orme —
[illegible] Smith, M. Johnson, E. Blowers
as Teachers,
The name of the Vicar
of the Parish is the Rev S. Adams,
The members of Parliament for

4

this Division are J. T. Paget Esqr
Liberal and A Pell Esqr Conservative
The President of the G. Baptist
Association is the Rev W Evans
of Leicester.
John Willis Esqr of Thorley
is the Architect and Mr Wm
Needham of Loughborough con-
tractor for this building,
The new plot of land
which the School rooms are built
on was purchased and given
by Mr J. Hanson Senr Bagworth
This was wrote by Geo Johnson
Secretary to the Sunday School on
July 20. 1885. Aged 20

THE PREACHER'S PLAN

For BARTON, BARLESTONE, BOSWORTH, BAGWORTH, &C.

From April to September 1885 inclusive.

PLACES	APRIL 5	APRIL 12	APRIL 19	APRIL 26	MAY 3	MAY 10	MAY 17	MAY 24	MAY 31	JUNE 7	JUNE 14	JUNE 21	JUNE 28
	m a e	m a e	m a e	m a e	m a e	m a e	m a e	m a e	m a e	m a e	m a e	m a e	m a e
BARTON	1 1	2 3	1 5	2 P	1 1	2 10	1 7	2 9	1 P	2 2	1 3	2 8	1 P
Wed.	M	1	1	2	M	1	2	1	2	M	1	1	
BOSWORTH.	1 10	2 9	1	2 2	1 6	2 8	1	2 2	1 1	2 11	1 4	2	1 7
Tues.		1		2		1							
CONGERSTONE.	12	2	8	8	7	2	3	10	12	8	1	4	5
Tues.			1				1						
BARLESTONE.	2 7	1 5	2	1 1	2 2	1 4	8	1 1	2 2	1 6	2 12	1	
Tues.	M	2	2	1	M	2	2	1	2	M	2	2	
BAGWORTH.	2 2	1 4	2 11	1 P	2 8	1 5	8 6	1 12	2 P	1 1	S P	1 11	2 P
Wed.		2		1		2			1				
NEWBOLD.	3	1	9	6	12	1	11	8	3	7	2 2	6	P
Tues.	2							2					
DESFORD.							2 2						
Wed.	1				2								
REFERENCES.	Ordinance at Bagworth		Church Meeting	Bosworth S. Sermons	Ordinance at Barlestone	Quarterly Collection	Quarterly Church Meeting			Ordinance at Bagworth	Newbold School Sermons	Church Meeting at Barlestone	Barlestone School Sermons.

PLACES	JULY 5	JULY 12	JULY 19	JULY 26	AUGUST 2	AUGUST 9	AUGUST 16	AUGUST 23	AUGUST 30	SEPTEMBER 6	SEPTEMBER 13	SEPTEMBER 20	SEPTEMBER 27
	m a e	m a e	m a e	m a e	m a e	m a e	m a e	m a e	m a e	m a e	m a e	m a e	m a e
BARTON	1 1	2 P	8 4	2 P	2		2 7	1 10	2 P	1 1	2 6	1 11	2 P
Wed.													
BOSWORTH.	1 12	2 10	8	2 2	2 6	1 P	2	1 1	2 2	1 9	2 5	1	2 2
Tues.													
CONGERSTONE.	3	2	7	12	2		8	9	4	5	2	7	10
Tues.													
BARLESTONE.	2 2	1 8	2	1 1	1 10	2 P	1	2 2	1 1	2 2	1 11	6	1 1
Tues.													
BAGWORTH.	2 7	1 9	2 8	1 P	1 1	2 P	1 12	2 6	1 P	2 8	1 8	8 5	1 P
Wed.													
NEWBOLD.	10	1	5	P	11	2	6	7	12	10	1	4	8
Tues.													
DESFORD.			1 1									2 2	
Wed.													
REFERENCES.	Ordinance at Barlestone		Church Meeting	Desford School Sermons	Ordinance at Bagworth	Barton School Sermons	Quarterly Church Meeting		Quarterly Collection	Ordinance at Barlestone.		Church Meeting at Barlestone	

M—Missionary Prayer Meeting.

P—Prayer Meeting.

S—Supply.

PREACHERS.

1 G. Needham, Barton.
2 J. R. Godfrey, Barlestone.
3 T. Deacon, Barton.
4 J. Compton, Newton.
5 W. Cramp, Newton.
6 E. Smith, Nailstone Wood.
7 G. Maides, Bosworth.
8 W. Bridget, Nailstone Wood.
9 A. Swann, Desford.
10 R. C. Chawner, Desford.
11 W. Banton, Bagworth.
12 J. Findley, Ibstock.

Preachers Plan

Inside the bottle was a Preachers Plan for Barton, Barlestone, Bosworth, Congerstone, and Bagworth. The information showed that in 1885 there were twelve preachers and seven churches in Barton in the Beans, Barlestone, Market Bosworth, Bagworth, Newbold Verdon, Desford and Congerstone. There was a Preachers Plan which indicates the rota arrangements for covering all the churches over a period of six months.

A copy of 'The Post' told of what life was like in those times. In the adverts, an 'original' Turkish bath, including shampoo could be had for a shilling in New Street, Leicester. Hair restorer was on special offer at one and six pence. The 'news of the day' told of the death of a foundry worker at Gimson and Company, in Humberstone Road, Leicester, after a heavy metal door fell on his legs.

A complete rundown of the contents of the Time Capsule are given in the diagram. This mine of bygone information has now been photocopied. The capsule was sealed with wax and consists of a glass jar. On the lid were the words, 'John Kilner Wakefield', and contains items shown in the key.

A cabinet was made to house the contents of the time capsule by Mr Peter Willett out of pine joists salvaged from the 1885 chapel while the demolition programme was in progress. The glazed cabinet houses assorted bricks— many of which bear their manufacturer's name— used in the building of the 1885 chapel.. The time capsule (Kilner jar) has been mounted as a centrepiece. No doubt the ingeniously recycled wood of the cabinet will stand the rigours of a further 100 years or more. The cabinet can now be seen on permanent display inside the lobby of the new church.

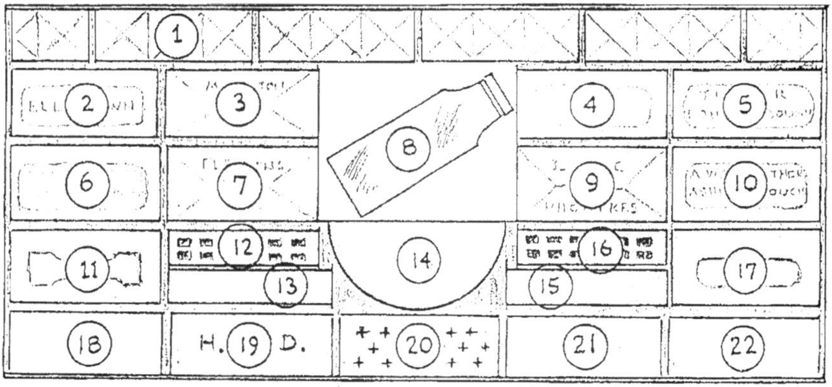

1. Pyramid shaped bricks from gable end of old chapel front.
2. Ellistown red facing brick 1885 used externally.
3. Marston common brick used in kitchen area.
4. Ellistown red facing brick (obverse side).
5. Tucker's common brick - used in Minister's Vestry 1885.
6 & 10. A Wain, Heather, Ashby De La Zouch, red facing brick 1885 used externally.
7. Flettons Ltd, common brick 1885, used internally in main chapel.
8. Time Capsule, found sealed within brickwork on left hand side of main entrance doors during demolition.
The glass jar is marked 'John Kilner Wakefield' on the lid, and contained the following items:
a) 3 Victorian 1 penny peices 1885.
b) A letter from Mr George S. Johnson, secretary to the Sunday School dated 20th July 1885. Six memorial stones were laid on 21st July 1885. The pastors were Rev. George Needham and J.R. Godfrey. Lay preachers and Deacons are also named. John Wills of Derby was the architect and Mr Wm Needham of Loughborough was the builder.
c) Laying of memorial stones programme.
d) The last Sunday School Anniversary hymn sheet held in the original chapel dated May 3rd 1885.
e) The Preacher's plan from April to September 1885.
f) The Leicester Daily Post newspaper price 1 penny.
g) The Freeman (Baptist newspaper).
h) The General Baptist Magazine.
9. London Brick Company Phorpres - a common brick used in kitchen area.
11 & 17. Blue damp proof bricks.
12 & 16. Ventilation bricks from Sunday School.
13 & 15. Tucker's of Loughborough from Minister's Vestry chimney breast.
14. Semi circular brick used to support floor joists in main chapel.
18 & 22. Sunday School facing bricks about 1885.
19. Red facing brick inscribed H.D.
20. Blue ventilation brick
21. Common used inside old chapel.

All the wood used in this frame, is wood from the old chapel.

Part of the memorial for the 1885 Chapel, showing salvaged bricks which contain the time capsule.

CHAPTER 34

BUILDING & FURNISHING THE NEW CHURCH

Timetable of Construction:

1) Demolition of the old church was completed on August 17th, 1995.
2) R.J.H. first set their stall out to build the new church when they moved on to the site on August 18th.
3) Peter Willett and Robert Holmes check the setting out on August 19.
4) Excavation for the foundations had started to be dug by August 21st.
5) Concrete foundations pumped in on September 1st.
6) The first blocks were laid on September 4th
7) Brickwork was done during September.
8) Up to roof level by October 13th.
9) Roof construction began on October 19th and tiling was completed on November 17th.
10) Drainage was started on December 5th.
11) Internal fittings— plastering, electrics, finishing off jobs, were done in January 1996.
12) Decorating was completed by February 27th.
13) Carpeting was laid on March 27th.
14) Opening ceremony of the new church was on April 20th, 1996.

By mid March the new building was complete and ready for the opening ceremony, to be performed on April 20th, 1996.

Foundations: note the heavvy steel reinforcement in the foundations.

Pumping in the concrete foundations from the car park, on Sept. 1st 1995

The first concrete blocks are laid – September 4th 1995.

Concrete floor beams are set in place.

The first brickwork gets underway.

Archway constructed for the Petal Window.

The Three Windows from the 1885 Chapel now overlook the Graveyard.

Ken Payne (Architect) on the left, and Roger Hemsley (Builder) enjoying a cup of tea.

A memorial has been erected in the lobby of the new (1996) chapel, in remembrance of the 1885 chapel. It was engraved by 90-year-old stone mason Mr W. H. Sawbridge of Ellistown.

A Welsh slate plaque reads simply:

IN MEMORY OF
CROSS HILLS BAPTIST
CHAPEL
1885 - 1995

Mr. W.H. Sawbridge, 90 year old stone-mason of Ellistown, who engraved the slate memorial plaque in the new Church.

The New Church and Memorial Garden.

Furnishing the New Church

By saving the suitable furniture from the 1885 chapel very little new furniture, with the exception of new church seating, had to be purchased. The following are some of the things salvaged from the old building. Antique items on the baptistry, i.e. the communion table and chairs; the flower stand, in memory of Mr. F.H. Whitmore; the lectern, in memory of Mr. 'Shirley' Gamble; also the replacement electric organ donated in memory of Mr. Clifford Farmer and his wife, Gladys.

All look splendid in their new surroundings, as does the old wall clock, which can be seen on the 1885 chapel photograph that also features the old oil lamps! A large cross, which now hangs in the church, was made out of old chapel timber by Mr John Hill, deacon.

The most expensive item on the furnishing programme bill was the new chairs. As funds were extremely low, it was initially decided to order about 20, and to help out with the cost, people were asked to donate half the price of a chair, which was about £25. This included a small name plaque, fixed on top of the chair, in memory of their loved ones.

The response was unbelievable. In the first two days 30 had been ordered, the total rapidly increasing to 40, 50, and by the opening of the church 60 had been delivered. Even then, 6 more were commissioned before a halt had to be called, there being no more accommodation space.

Part of the New DIY Kitchen assembled by members.

Kitchen Furnishing

The next biggest furnishing problem encountered was the kitchen. This had not been included in the original building contract to keep down the costs of a limited budget, as only the bare basics could be afforded. But a very generous donation from a member, plus taking advantage of a half-price winter sale at a local M.F.I. store, meant the whole of the required cabinets and fittings could be purchased.

Subsequently came the D.I.Y. installation of the units, carried out in fine fashion by certain members of the church! New crockery was purchased and a very good secondhand cooker and water boiler were donated to complete the fittings.

The carpeting was fitted professionally, and after the church was given a good clean-up, all was ready for the 'off'! To everyone, this was an amazing achievement, as no-one ever imagined the building would be completed fully for the 'Grand opening Ceremony' on April 20th, 1996.

CHAPTER 35

THE OPENING OF THE NEW CROSS HILLS BAPTIST CHURCH

CROSS HILLS BAPTIST CHURCH

TO THE RESIDENTS OF BAGWORTH & THORNTON

WE INVITE YOU TO THE
OPENING SERVICE
OF THE NEW CHURCH
SATURDAY 20th APRIL 1996
COMMENCING AT 3.30pm

A SPECIAL SERVICE OF THANKS
FOR THE NEW BUILDING AND FOR
THE SUPPORT GIVEN BY BOTH COMMUNITIES

DEDICATION & MESSAGE REVD. PETER GRANGE EMBA
WORSHIP LED BY PASTOR GARRY KELLY

JOIN WITH US ON THIS SPECIAL DAY
AS WE CELEBRATE
WITH SONG AND PRAISE

REFRESHMENTS AFTER THE SERVICE
ALL RESIDENTS OF THORNTON & BAGWORTH
ARE WELCOME,
PLEASE NOTE SEATING IS RESTRICTED
THEREFORE THIS SERVICE IS RESTRICTED TO
THE LOCAL COMMUNITY ONLY

SUNDAY 21st APRIL
10.30am - Revd. Eddie Pilling
5.00pm - Revd. Bob Stephen

YOU ARE ALWAYS WELCOME AT OUR SUNDAY MORNING SERVICES 10.30am

The March

Grand opening day was on Saturday April 20th 1996. It was a proud moment, the culmination of much hard work by members. They could hardly believe that the brand new church was about to be opened at last, with the blessing of the Lord.

It was a glorious sunny afternoon as two separate contingents assembled with their Banners of 'Cross Hills Baptists' at the top of the hills at Bagworth and Thornton.

At a precise moment the two parties set off down the gradients on their respective march, so that both parties converged on Cross Hills

Cross Hills
Baptist Church

Celebration & Thanksgiving
Service
for the opening of
the new church

20th April 1996

Conducted By
Revd. Peter Grange

"Lift up your heads, O you gates;
lift them up, you ancient doors,
that the King of glory may come in."
Psalm 24 v 7

Pastor - Garry Kelly - 01455 842312
Secretary - Robert Holmes - 01530 230624
Treasurer - Peter Willett - 01530 230670

Cross Hills in the centre of the picture from the top of Thornton Hill.

church car park at the same time. The Lord Mayor of Hinckley & Bosworth, Counc. Joyce Crooks, arrived to start the official opening ceremony, the timing of which is shown.

Thornton members prepare for 'The March' on the 'Opening Day'.

All members – Bagworth and Thornton – meet at the 'New Church'.

At the opening of the New Church on 20th April 1996: Left to right; George Farmer (Life Deacon); Garry Kelly (Pastor); Lynda Kelly; Roger Hemsley (Builder); Peter Willett (Treasurer); Robert Holmes (Secretary); Ken Payne (Architect); Rev. Peter Grange (Area Superintendent); Mrs Grange.

A gathering of members after the opening.

View of inside the New Church.

Note the re-use of the balustrading, Altar rail, table donated by Arthur Orme, Baptistry chairs donated by Mr. Reg Willett, and petal window & side window.

Time Table for Cross Hills Baptist Church Opening Service Proceeded as follows:

Saturday, April 20, 1996.

10.00am until 12.00 noon, the doors were first opened to the public for viewing.
12.30pm Church closed for preparation.
3.00pm Marchers arrive at the top of both hills (Thornton and Bagworth ends)
3.20pm Hinckley and Bosworth Borough Council Mayor Counc Joyce Crooks arrived with guests.
3.30pm Marchers and non-marchers arrive at church and are welcomed in.
3.50pm Church doors locked (with congregation inside.)
Kenneth Payne (Architect) and Roger Hemsley (Builder) hand keys to Lord Mayor;
Lord Mayor hands keys to Mr George Farmer, Life Deacon, who unlocks and opens the church doors.
4.00pm The opening service conducted by Rev. Peter Grange, (Area Superintendent).
5.00pm Refreshments and a time to view the church.

To complete a wonderful monumental weekend to celebrate the opening of the new church, a Celebration and Thanksgiving Service was held on Sunday, April 21 1996 at 10.30am by Rev. Eddie Pilling. The 5.00pm service was conducted by Rev. Bob Stephen. A special hymn sheet was issued for the occasion.

The Leicester Mercury covered the opening ceremony, when more than 120 villagers from Thornton and Bagworth attended the opening, with three special services.

Cross Hills
Baptist Church

Celebration & Thanksgiving
Service
10.30am

21st April 1996

Conducted By
Revd. Eddie Pilling

Pastor - Garry Kelly - 01455 842312
Secretary - Robert Holmes - 01530 230524
Treasurer - Peter Willett - 01530 230670

First Baptism

On Sunday, April 28th, 1996, Mrs Hilda Lovitt was baptised in a full immersion ceremony at Cross Hills, conducted by Pastor Gary Kelly.

She said, *'It's a lovely new church, very peaceful and it was a lovely day. I was the first to be baptised in the new church.'*

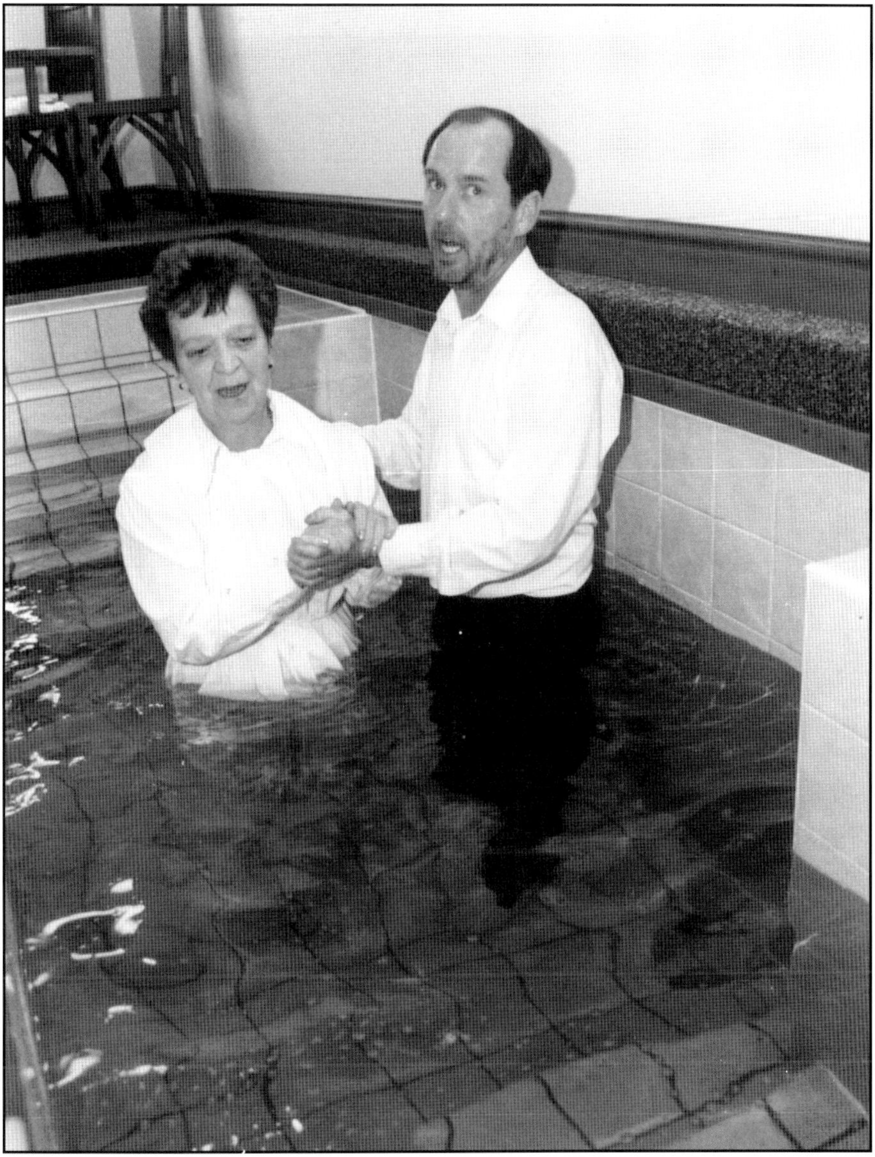

Pastor Garry Kelly uses the new Baptistry for the first time.
Photograph – courtesy of 'Leicester Mercury'

CHAPTER 36

MINISTERS AND PASTORS THROUGH THE YEARS

Barton and Cross Hills from 1796:

Jacob Brewin	1797-1816
John Green	1817-1823
John Derry	1824-1852
Joseph Cotton	1843-1855
Joseph Holroyd	1857-1863
Edward Bott	1852-1864
Driver	1864-1865
W. Hill	1865-1871
E. W. Cantrell	1867-1870
William Jarrom	1870-1874
H. Wood	1871-1875
James Brown	1872-1873
James Greenwood	1874-1879
G. Needham	1876-1888
W. Hubbard	1880-1884
E. Gilbert	1881-1883
J. R. Godfrey	1885-1910
G. E. Payne	1888-1902
Rev. J. D. Humphreys	1902-1907
Rev. J.R. Godfrey	1904-1912
Rev. B. Owen	1908-1910
Rev. C. Palmer	1910-1916
P. Flanders.	1915
Rev. T. C. Darvell	1913-1923
Rev. E. A. Martin	1916
Pastor Sims	1935-1936
Rev. R. D. Browne	
Rev. E. J. Garnham	1920-1954
Rev. J. Gardiner	1954-1960
Rev. P. Peel	1963-1968
Rev. J. Noddings	1973-1977
Rev. Alan Webb	1980-1989
Pastor Rev. Garry Kelly (for Cross Hills only)	1991-

All the above, except Pastor Garry Kelly, ministered for the 'Group of Churches' and most lived in either the Barton Manse or the Barlestone Manse.

CHAPTER 37

CONCLUSION

IT'S BEEN A LONG, TRIUMPHANT JOURNEY

We have travelled a long eventful journey together: it is over 260 years since the great pioneers of the Baptist Movement started out on their triumphant mission for Jesus Christ. For much of the time it has been a tough, testing battle for them. These brave people and their families had to endure unimaginable persecution and prejudice. Not only were they despised and attacked by atheists, but also by people who regarded themselves as members of the Anglican Church. But even when they were spat upon and reviled, their vision in the cause of God stayed right on track.

We have read of certain key people who were at the forefront when the New Connexion of General Baptists was formed. There were doubtless others, just as important, just as dedicated, who never wanted or received due recognition for the work they did— wives, brothers, aunts, farm workers. However small a part was played, it represented an essential piece of the jigsaw which was needed to complete the whole picture during those difficult times.

The Barton Society was formed in 1743, and became the central hub around which a host of satellite chapels were to spring forth. Eighteen years after Samuel Deacon II raised the Standard of the Cross in Bagworth and Thornton in 1796, Cross Hills church was built. It had taken all those long eighteen years to find anyone willing to sell the land on which to erect a permanent branch. The Dissenters had not yet been accepted by the general public or the Anglican Church. People did not want to be seen to encourage these upstarts by selling them ground in their villages, so the Bagworth branch eventually managed to settle for a piece of land midway between Thornton and Bagworth, where it is today.

As a direct result of the suffering and struggle of these brave pioneers it is possible today to visit Cross Hills, to bring the children, to worship God without fear of reprisal or prejudice from fellow man. In this modern day of 1998 the Anglican Church and the Baptist Church have more in common in teaching the Word of God. Indeed, some other denominations now also happily work hand in hand in the common cause of worship. A far cry from the struggle back in those early days of trailblazers such as Whitefield, Lady Selina, David Taylor and the Deacon family, to name but a few.

Today, many descendants of the characters you have read about, still live happily in Bagworth and Thornton. Good old family names that survive the centuries in virtually the same location. Some of these people will find a taste of the lifestyles of their forebears, which they can then hand down to their heirs in the form of this book for posterity.

Stories by word of mouth become lost or distorted over the years. Memories become blurred like the dewy mists of a spring morning.

The purpose of this book is to set a permanent record of the work of our ancestors with regards to Cross Hills, and to bring it all to life with a few of their unique tales. The building of the new church in 1996 marked yet another phase in the story of Cross Hills. We have only just entered this new phase as we near the millennium. The authors hope that in another 200 years someone else will bring the story of Cross Hills yet again up to date, and keep Samuel Deacon II's 1796 standard flying in Thornton and Bagworth in the name of God. Until that time, we will close the book in the knowledge that our great pioneers of the Baptist Movement can rest assured that they have done a worthy job in the eyes of the Lord.

Praise God, From whom all blessings flow;
Praise Him, all creatures here below;
Praise Him Above, ye heavenly host;
Praise Father, Son, and Holy Ghost.

Amen

FEAR NOT

1) Fear not, He is with you,
Do not be afraid,
To help and cheer you
This promise He made;
When you feel downhearted
Just trust Him and pray,
Fear not He is with you
He is with you today.

2) Fear not, He is near you,
Just reach out your hand,
Just tell Him your troubles
And He'll understand;
Then ask Him to guide you
Along life's way,
Fear not, He is with you
He is with you today.

3) Fear not, He is with you
In joy and in pain
And He will prove faithful
Again and again;
When shadows are falling
And life's near the end,
He'll be waiting for you
Your Saviour and friend.

4) Fear not, you shall see Him
Then all will be clear,
Your troubles will vanish
Along with your tears;
Then you shall be happy,
Your tears wiped away,
Fear not, you shall see Him,
You shall see Him one day.

Lynda Joy Kelly